CHRISTOPHER FILDES

A
CITY
SPECTATOR

Bulls, Bears, Booms and Boondoggles

as chronicled in

CITY & SUBURBAN

Edited by Martin Vander Weyer

NICHOLAS BREALEY
PUBLISHING

LONDON

First published by
Nicholas Brealey Publishing in 2004

3–5 Spafield Street
Clerkenwell, London
EC1R 4QB, UK
Tel: +44 (0)20 7239 0360
Fax: +44 (0)20 7239 0370

100 City Hall Plaza, Suite 501
Boston
MA 02108, USA
Tel: (888) BREALEY
Fax: (617) 523 3708

http://www.nbrealey-books.com

ISBN 1-85788-336-5

British Library Cataloguing in Publication Data
A catalogue record for this book is available from the
British Library.

Printed in Finland by WS Bookwell.

CONTENTS

PREFACE

'Easy reading is damn hard writing.'
Nathaniel Hawthorne

For more than a quarter of a century, Christopher Fildes has delighted his readers with a unique combination of fine writing and pithy comments on life in the City. In his case wit and wisdom go together. The articles in this collection tell the story of the development of the City of London as an international financial centre, from the days when Siegmund Warburg was changing the nature of financial contracts, through the revolution of Big Bang in 1986, to the 'Wimbledonisation' of the City. His writing covers also the extraordinary ups and downs of the British economy – the Great Inflation of the 1970s, the Thatcher revolution of the 1980s, and the new framework for monetary stability of the 1990s.

Throughout it all, Christopher Fildes has remained a sharp and perceptive observer of both institutions and people – a true City Spectator. His analysis of exchange rates – based on the negroni index – reminds us that they are market prices, not totems. His descriptions of the many colourful characters who worked in the City, their stories, the places where they ate and drank, the buildings they inhabited, all convey the ups and downs of that extraordinary community known as the City of London. Christopher Fildes combines a real affection for the City – both old and new – with a readiness to be trenchantly critical when the occasion demands, criticism which is all the more effective when it comes from a knowledgeable friend. As he concludes about the City, 'its greatest mistake would be to take its own success for granted'.

Whether you agree with him or not in his judgements about both institutions and people, you will certainly find something to enjoy and savour in this fascinating collection of articles. As Johnson might have said, if a man is tired of the City of London then he is tired of working life. There is no risk of that with Christopher Fildes. And if a reader is tired of reading Fildes, then he is too tired to read at all.

Mervyn King
Bank of England, August 2004

INTRODUCTION

The City traces itself back to the giants Gog and Magog, derives its street plan from Roman Londinium, contributed the Lord Mayor who knifed Wat Tyler, gave refuge to the Five Members when they fled from Charles I and was called by Clarendon the sink of all the ill-humour in the kingdom. Independent-minded and awkward, it seems to have been here forever, but it could not have lasted as long or as well as it has if it had not kept changing. It has always been a wonderful place to study human nature.

When I first arrived there, in the palaeolithic era, the City ran to top hats and gentlemen's hours. On its bomb sites, the post-war architects had done their best or worst. At a dinner in the Mansion House, the Prince of Wales addressed them: 'Say what you like against the Luftwaffe, they only knocked it down.'

They certainly had. In the second great fire of London, which left its historic Square Mile or much of it in ruins, the old City of merchants and warehouses – Dickens's City – was destroyed and lost for ever. The City of bankers and brokers survived, to live as best it could in a world which had moved on. Its choices, then and afterwards, mirrored the nation's. Had it lost an empire, was it looking for a role, and could it hope to find one?

You could say that its inhabitants found a place of their own. In this tired soil they grew a beanstalk of a business which found new ways of financing the world, rewarded some of its denizens grossly, and earned so much money abroad as to be the nation's most improbably successful export industry. Along the way they lost their hats and took to working longer hours. There have been other losses which are harder to measure.

I had the good fortune to watch all this happening, and for the past 20 years I have had the two best seats in the house, by courtesy of *The Spectator* and *The Daily Telegraph*. David Kynaston, the City's historian, was kind enough to call me the financial journalist who would most closely follow the domestic habits of the City and its inhabitants. I saw them in parlours and alleyways and luncheon rooms, in formative moments, in moments of crisis and of relaxation. They made change, and change overtook them.

City and Suburban, my *Spectator* column, took its name from a handicap at Epsom: I had forgotten that John Betjeman had given the same name to his own column in *The Spectator*, and by time I remembered this, guiltily, it was too late. I maintained that the name was suggested to me by my racing correspondent, Captain Threadneedle. He was joined by other specialists, such as I. K. Gricer (railways) and Jumbo Speedbird (aviation)

If they were not to be found in the *Financial Times*'s pink acreages, so much the better. They reflected my belief that finance is a specialised branch of human nature, and Walter Bagehot's belief, expressed in *Lombard Street*, his classic of the Victorian City, that a writer on money must blame himself if he is not understood. Writing a column like this was like writing a letter and posting it in a hollow tree. I was happy to find that the letters were being retrieved and enjoyed.

Those paleolithic top hats had been part of a uniform. City editors once kept them on shelves in their offices, ready to cram on their heads if they had to go round to the Bank of England and talk to the Governor. I gave one of the hats a safe haven. Bill-brokers still wore them. They walked round the banks, borrowed the spare money in the system and invested it to make a living. Lord Radcliffe had reported that if they did not exist, God would not have found it necessary to invent them, but they were a spirited club and, in a City of concentric circles, close to the Bank of England at the centre. Kenneth Whitaker, who gave the City's best lunches, put in a bid for the Queen's undertakers: 'Synergy, dear boy,' he told me. 'It's something else we can do with our hats.' The theft of Lord Clarendon's hat, snatched from his head as he went on his rounds, was an omen.

The innermost circle of all, and the grandest club, was the Accepting Houses Committee, and its members were the merchant bankers. For generations, their families – Rothschilds, Barings, Hambros – had made the local weather. When Lord Cromer, who held one of the Barings' six peerages, went to the Bank of England as Governor, his crusty uncles and cousins resented it, muttering that young Rowley needn't expect to have his place kept warm. The great families had come from Frankfurt and Bremen and Copenhagen to a City whose doors had been open to them. Now their ascendancy was challenged by a newcomer, who had been driven from home by the menace of Hitler. This was Siegmund Warburg. Cultured, committed, professional, formidable, he made the weather bracing.

At different times in its long history, an open and competitive City had settled down to be a City of clubs and cartels. In bad times, this was its defensive reaction. Warburg, more than anyone, opened it up again. His bank took on the establishment, beat it and, finally and fatally, joined it. Along the way the new thinkers had hit upon a transforming discovery: the City could do business in any currency for any country. Sterling's troubles, which were the British economy's troubles, need no longer hold it back.

The gold sovereign had been a touchstone. For a quarter of a millennium, the pound had held its value, faltering only in three great European wars. Then, in the half-century of peace that followed, it lost 98 per cent of its purchasing power. One sterling crisis after another – as much a part of the British scene, said John Kenneth Galbraith, as tarts in Piccadilly – blew governments off course or, if you were on the other side of the debate, brought them up against reality.

The City escaped it. A banker going abroad on holiday with more than £50 in his pocket was liable to arrest and imprisonment, but he could arrange for his clients to finance themselves in other currencies, without controls or limits. City skills and offshore dollars made a winning combination. Banks rushed in from every direction to tap this new market. The Bank of England made them welcome. Soon there were more American banks in London than in New York. With them came an influx of talent. They had sent their best and brightest.

Michael Von Clemm, innovator and polymath, resented the City's preference for nursery food and backed the Roux brothers, chefs to the Rothschilds. Soon the Roux restaurants twinkled with Michelin stars. In the wasteland of London's docks, Von Clemm prospected a site for his bank's back office and thought that it would suit the front office better. From this gleam in his eye grew the tall financial factories of Canary Wharf, four miles to the east of the old Square Mile. He moved his own office further and further west. Like a true international banker, he liked to be within range of the airport.

Under pressure from without and in response to new realities, the City's cartels and clubs imploded. The Stock Exchange's Big Bang was the loudest implosion of all. For years the Exchange had fought a rearguard action in defence of its members and their way of life and scale of charges. In the end, armed by technology, competition broke its walls down.

Once stocks could be traded on screens, at the touch of a button, the Exchange's trading floor had lost its monopoly and, soon, its reason for existence. Now, said a Bank of England director, London could have a securities business to match its international businesses in banking and insurance. The death of exchange control, that temporary wartime expedient which after 40 years had begun to look permanent, meant that money was free once more to flow in and out of London and around the world, and that bankers could take their holidays abroad without fear of arrest.

Sterling's last test and the City's longest day were still to come. The pound, unwisely (as I thought and wrote) fastened to Germany's wagon through a ramshackle framework of European currencies, became unhitched. A merchant bank's treasurer, as the waves of sellers rolled towards him, reflected that it must have been like this at Rorke's Drift. A combatant in the Bank of England, asked when the Bank had last raised its rate twice in a day, told me: '1914. Standard procedure for declaring war on Germany.' A bank chairman muttered that if it happened again he would call in the auditors. A bill-broker, facing ruin, went home for a bath and a stiff drink, to be told that the experiment was over. Soon enough it became clear that we were better off without it.

Memories such as these kept doubts alive in the City when it was told that its future and Britain's must lie with Europe's newly minted single currency. If it were left outside, so the story went, Frankfurt or Paris would take all its business and grass would grow in Cornhill. Setting five tests which had to be passed before we could contemplate joining, the Chancellor of the day included its effect on the City's international markets. That, in its way, was a compliment, but when the euro was born, the City's response was to make markets in it.

This, though, was a new kind of City and its old leaders, or most of them, had been outpaced. At Big Bang, the partners in all but one of the Stock Exchange's leading firms gave up control and took their money out. It could still be seen from the air, having been reinvested in swimming pools (said Margaret Reid, Big Bang's historian) all along the North Downs. Bill-brokers no longer exist and God seems to agree with Lord Radcliffe.

More shocking has been the eclipse of the merchant bankers, for so long the City's aristocracy. Barings, in its third century, was brought down by a fraud and by its own greed and folly. Other families needed no prompting to make for the exit. The Swiss owners of Siegmund Warburg's bank, which was once backed to take on the world, have scratched his name off. A dynastic chieftain, David Montagu, once asked me which merchant banks were for sale. When I ducked the question back to him, he told me: 'I should think they all are. This one certainly is. All of them, I suppose, except Rothschilds.' He was right to the letter.

Some of the City's institutions have found it hard to adjust. The Stock Exchange, having lost its monopoly and three successive chief executives, then lost its nerve and tried to merge with Deutsche Börse on terms which amounted to surrender. It was lucky to escape. Arrogance and introspection nearly wrecked Lloyd's of London. The Bank of England, which saw early and clearly that the City had to live by competition, has been granted its independence but told to concentrate on monetary policy. This in itself was a radical change for the better, but the City's mother hen has had her wings clipped and some of the chicks may turn out to be cuckoos.

In all this change, human nature is the constant. Hence my law of the financial cycle, which says that disasters happen when the last man who can remember what happened last time has retired. Hold tight and watch the wheel come round.

PART I

CITY

CHAPTER ONE

BULLS, BEARS, BOOMS AND BUSTS

White-knuckle rides on the world markets – and logging the dot.coms off

I have to admit that my approach to the markets owes something to Eeyore: 'Good morning. If it is a good morning. Which I doubt.' I may miss some of the fun, but it kept me sane (and might have helped to keep my readers solvent) in one of the great swelling bubbles of stock market history, when we were led to believe that information technology was transforming our lives – and, which was not the same thing, that it could make us all rich. It certainly seemed to do wonders for the bright sparks who tacked on '.com' to their companies' names. Grave financial statesmen were carried away and encouraged us to believe that the new technology had ushered in a new paradigm. This seemed to mean that the laws of economics had been abolished in our time and in our favour. Chance would have been a fine thing, but I was right to doubt it.

High and dry

The great City crash must be nearer than we think. Witness the exchange between two of the City's most potent forces: one, just about its biggest wine merchant; the other, just about its grandest merchant bank, whose name is good for billions. The bank ordered a case of champagne. Two months later, no champagne had arrived. Commotion at the bank, stone faces at the wine merchant: they would not deliver without cash in advance. One way or another, there is a crisis of liquidity. (30 March 1985)

The bright side

The Aids boom shows the stock market in uninhibited form. Any share in any company which might have anything to offer in dealing with the plague becomes the hottest property. First come the pharmaceutical companies, respected names like Glaxo and Wellcome, whose researchers may enable them, years ahead, to offer some kind of treatment: the Japanese have bought their shares by the truckload. Then London International Group, which at other times does not like to be known as the nation's dominant supplier of contraceptive sheaths. That is not a research-based, technologically advanced product in the same class as Wellcome's, but the share price still responds. Now BTP, which stands for British Tar Products. Is tar good for Aids? Well, BTP has let it be known that it has a fluid in which the Aids virus cannot live. I should not think the virus can live in sulphuric acid, either, but that is no reason to buy ICI. The BTP shares, though, went through the roof. What a funny coincidence that BTP has a bid on its hands.

At least it all shows the market's propensity for looking on the bright side. Jerry Goodman, who writes as 'Adam Smith', tells in *Supermoney* of a group of Wall Street analysts in the heartland of General Motors. They were disturbed, presciently, about indications of decline in America's smokestack industries. They were shown one production line whose manager explained, in despair, that 14 per cent of the staff used heroin. An analyst brightened up: '14 per cent? Jeez! Who makes the syringes?' (7 March 1987)

Unauthorised version

I cannot but giggle when Merrill Lynch announces that it has lost $250 million on bonds – because of a dealer's 'unauthorised trading'. Poor old unauthorised trading, the standard scapegoat, trotted out once more! When shall we hear a bank or broker announce that its trading, though unauthorised, has brought in a whacking great profit? My friend Herbie of the Last National Bank of Boot Hill made the point when someone else's debacle was blamed on unauthorised trading: 'This means that nobody authorised the guy to get it wrong.' (9 May 1987)

Roll on, quiescence

The 'Black Monday' global stock market crash had occurred on 19 October.

Confidence, enthusiasm, panic, funk – that (I was saying) is the market cycle, with its worst moment when enthusiasm gives way to panic. Tim Congdon, the Sage of Shearsons, prefers to quote the Victorian banker Lord Overstone: 'The state of trade can be divided [so Lord Overstone testified, 150 years ago] into successive conditions of quiescence, improvement, growing confidence, prosperity, excitement, overtrading, convulsion, pressure, stagnation, and distress, ending again in quiescence.' All I can add is, roll on quiescence. (31 October 1987)

Vision and boundless hope and optimism – there's a lot of it about

Here on Wall Street, these are heady days. The world's biggest economy, as valued by its stock market, is worth a half as much again as it was 21 months ago, and everyone wants to be part of it. Sales of mutual funds, the little man's way in, look set to double the figures for last year, when stocks were (of course) cheaper. Fund managers appear on the cover of *Time* magazine. The last big bears, at Morgan Stanley, have gone back into the woods. Shares with high-tech names and no earnings sell like hot properties. Americans are better off, their pay packets are fatter (on Wall Street, some of them, gargantuan) but prices in the shops have yet to follow. The recovery is heading for its seventh year, with Alan Greenspan at the Federal Reserve looking down upon it like Minerva's owl.

The scene is one of vision and boundless hope and optimism. Such are the words of Professor Charles Amos Dice, as preserved in John Kenneth Galbraith's *The Great Crash* – his account of the collective madness that swept over Wall Street at the end of the 1920s and brought on its greatest boom and bust. I brought it with me, thinking (on Gwendolen Fairfax's lines) that one should always have something sensational to read on the plane. Galbraith argues that such frenzies – like the South Sea Bubble or the house boom that closed the 1980s – come at the end of a prosperous time, when people too readily believe that it will always be like this, only better. Perhaps the all-wise Mr Greenspan has abolished the business cycle, or at any rate its down side. At such a time investors, and lenders too, can see the rewards more clearly than the risks. I dare say there are more rewards to come, but to me the great bull market of the 1990s has begun to look risky. (19 October 1996)

Bah! Bubble!

I have always sympathised with Scrooge – he stood for so much that was characteristic of the old City – so I enjoyed Alan Greenspan's appearance as a spectre at the markets' Christmas party, crying 'Bah! Bubble!' Those few unkind words from the chairman of the US Federal Reserve – 'inflated, exuberant, irrational' – went down like crumbs of indigestible cheese.

Two months ago when I was in New York, the Wall Street party was just getting into its stride. The world's biggest economy, as valued by its stock market, was worth half as much again as it had been two years earlier, fortunes had been earned or made and new investors were still piling in. Those hopes were dupes, but as I said: 'At such a time investors can see the rewards more clearly than the risks. I dare say there are more rewards to come but to me the great bull market of the 1990s has begun to look risky.' Now the sage of the Fed has his eye on the risks. It will not make either of us popular, but as our old City friend used to growl: 'It's enough for a man to mind his own business.' (14/21 December 1996)

Something must be done. Let's think of something

It could be worse. The markets have tumbled, Russia has defaulted, bankers and investors count their losses and wonder where the next ones are coming from, but we have thus far been spared official statements designed to restore confidence by reassuring us that everything is quite all right. These are always the signals to rush for the exits. Instead we have the next worst thing, which is the spectacle of finance ministers, central bank governors and their supporting cast of bag carriers and sherpas hurrying to meet each other and to think of something that they or their spokesmen can subsequently announce. They are tempted at such times to take initiatives. As Sir Humphrey Appleby suggested to Jim Hacker, 'Something must be done. This is something. We must therefore do it.' (19 September 1998)

Paradigms regained

The West's markets have risen so far and for so long that they are full of professionals who believe that markets always do this. (Amateurs, too, of course.) Willing to be of help, I offer them some precepts from my Bad Investment Guide. Markets, so they need to know, do not move in straight lines. They overdo things in both directions. As a rule they fall more sharply than they rise, for bubbles expand slowly and burst quickly. There is no more seductive promise in markets than the magic words, 'This time it's different.' (The American version of this is, or was, 'It's a new paradigm', meaning that economic laws have been suspended for the markets' benefit.) A cruder assurance can suggest that there is a wall of new money approaching the markets with nowhere else to go. People will always find homes for their money and, for that matter, ways of losing it, but when there is plenty of it about, they become less choosy. The The rule of thumb laid down by my mentor Sir Patrick Sergeant is that markets retrace their footsteps by going one-third of the way in the opposite direction. (26 September 1998)

Sibley's Law: this time the banks choose a hedge

The crash of US-based hedge fund Long-Term Capital Management, which had employed Nobel Laureate mathematicians to devise its trading formulae, briefly threatened to throw the whole international banking system into crisis.

I know I should keep a straight face, but the spectacle of banks finding new ways to lose money never fails to tickle me. Their ingenuity is breathtaking. Sometimes they lend to countries they could not find on a map, or emerging markets, as they were called before they submerged again. Sometimes they stay at home and collect unfinished office blocks or country houses where the eye of faith had conjured up hotels and golf courses. Look at them now as they come over with their hands up and admit their exposure to Long-Term Capital Management, the hedge fund. This swashbuckling performer, playing the markets with its bankers' money, swashed for a year or two but has now buckled. The Untied Bank of Switzerland thinks it prudent to provide against losses of £400 million. Dresdner Bank thought that £80 million will do. As for Barclays, still smarting from having lost £250 million in Russia, it is putting an extra $300 million into the pot but hopes to get it back.

The banks have turned on what used to be a sixpence. In July Sir Brian Pitman was complaining that Lloyds, his bank, would soon have £6 billion of excess capital and must find a use for it. Banks left and right have been searching for something to keep their capital busy, looking further afield for high returns or just spending their money on buying each other. They will now find out whether their cherished systems of risk appraisal are any better than a working memory and a good sense of smell. They will be reminded of the law laid down by that worldly banker Nicholas Sibley, and quoted here from time to time. Giving capital to a bank, so he said, is like giving a gallon of beer to a drunk: you know what will come of it, but you can't know which wall he will choose. I never thought that, this time, the banks would choose a hedge. (3 October 1998)

Baring crisis

I am sorry to learn that Berkeley Playhouse, the lap-dancing club, has gone bust, if that is the word I am looking for. Berkeley was one of last year's more sporting new share issues and I was sent a prospectus. In the margin of each right-hand page there was a picture of a girl, presumably the same girl, because if you riffled through the pages rapidly she would appear to take her clothes off. This must be an indicator for my Bad Investment (or Divestment) Guide. So often in investment, as in life, the tease is better than the strip. (7 November 1998)

Very lastminute

Sauntering to market this week is lastminute, most stylish of the dot.com stocks. Martha Lane Fox, whose baby this is, has been charming City editors across the lunch tables, doubtless reserved at the very last moment on favourable terms. This is lastminute's idea. It will let restaurants and theatres and airlines sell off their last few free places at clearance-sale prices. Lastminute will not be priced like that. The talking figure is £400 million, though its revenues are modest and its profits, as yet, non-existent. You have to buy the idea. I grumpily wonder how many customers will be content to take last-minute chances and how many of them will use lastminute when they do. The internet, so we are constantly told, is making markets transparent and will certainly enable us to trawl around for cheaper air fares without waiting to see what lastminute comes up with. If you are thinking of buying the shares, leave it late and hope for a price cut. (4 March 2000)

Dot.coms go up in smoke, cash is the best fire break, keep close to it now

We must go on learning in life, and backing dot.com companies has its own lessons. They do not, so we find, have price–earnings ratios (no earnings) or discounted cash flow (it flows out), but they have burn rates. These measure the pace at which they are getting through money: 'Our burn rate is £50,000 a week.' Or 'We are in great shape, we're at 90 per cent of burn rate' — meaning that they had budgeted to run out of money in September but now look as if they can last out for the rest of the year. Then they would plan to bring in new investors who, inspired by the company's potential, would add fuel to the fire. This worked well as long as they kept coming but now they, too, have got burned and the conflagration is spreading. Boo.com's burn rate has consumed it, others have postponed their appointments with the new investors — possibly for ever — and even the Prudential's Egg has had to be put on the back burner.

You would need to be older than most of the dot.com promoters to have seen markets reverse themselves so dramatically. In two or three months, shares like theirs have lost half their value. Only a month ago, they could still claim to be paper rich but cash skint, owning stakes in highly valued businesses but still bringing their socks home to Mum to be washed. Some of them will now turn out to be paper poor, too.

It is the oldest story of all. Cash is the lifeblood of any business. There are times when credit will do just as well, for, as the authors of *Refer to Drawer* point out, credit is only the Latin for 'he believes it'. Then belief is overstretched and, when it goes, cash goes too. Cash is the best fire break. Keep close to it now. (27 May 2000)

Cul-de-sac.com

If you want to read someone's excursus on 'Whither the dot.com economy', you may have to fall back on mine. Don't try The Street.com.uk, which has turned out to be more of a cul-de-sac. It was launched in the spring with the cheery assurance that its electronic City pages would put paid to paper and ink, but it now joins the lengthening list of dot.coms which seemed a good idea at the time. Easier.com, which traded houses over the internet, has decided to quit while it still has cash in the bank. Most of the others ran out and could raise no more. Their burn rates (their way of measuring the pace at which they got through money) consumed them. Running out of money is always and everywhere fatal to businesses, and some of these had nothing more going for them than the dot in their name, but their fate suggests that the old economy still has some fight in it. Paper and ink are still with us and so is s-commerce, the S, as you will recall, standing for shops. (25 November 2000)

When a lovely flame dies, soap gets in your eyes and you lose a trillion dollars

How swiftly a bubble bursts, and how finally. The rainbow-coloured sphere expands before our eyes, and at the next moment they are full of soap. Nothing is gained by trying to put it together again. One year ago the dot.com bubble burst. The new, electronic economy, though doubtless cleverer and more productive than the old economy, proved to be subject to the same old laws, beginning with the law of gravity. In London, at this time last year, the spirited Martha Lane Fox was bringing lastminute to market. ('If you are thinking of buying the shares,' I said, 'leave it late and hope for a price cut.' You can buy them now at an 85 per cent discount to the offer price.) A month later I was wondering whether the new technology had found a way of letting a bubble down gently. Apparently not. Dot.coms ran out of money and burned up, and the suppliers of their technology took to issuing profit warnings. In New York, the Nasdaq market, which had been the new technology's home territory, managed to lose more than half its value.

By now these losses extend to a trillion (that is to say, a million million) dollars. Even by the standards of the world's biggest economy, that is quite a lot of money to lose. It affects the behaviour of the people who have lost it. They spend and borrow and invest less, and save more. If they are banks, of course, they lend less. Some people and some banks run out of money. The central bank's legendary chairman celebrates his seventy-fifth birthday and looks Delphic. If the markets had invested less blind faith in him, they might not now have soap in their eyes. (10 March 2001)

Bigger fools

Boo.com was a short-lived London-based online fashion retailer founded by two Swedes, poet Ernst Malmsten and model Kajsa Leander, and briefly valued at £200 million.

The Swedes at boo.com were told that their finances were in disorder and that their kit did not work, but they brushed this aside: 'I'd banned all talk of failure and delay as defeatist.' So boo to the doubter who asked if they bought their own suits on the internet. They ran boo.com like a multinational on speed. They wondered if they had outgrown J. P. Morgan. They festooned themselves with expensive advisers, some of whom (Morgan included) were mugs enough to take payment in shares. The game would be to bring boo.com to market, when it would soon be worth more than $1 billion and make its backers rich. Can all this have happened last year? It seems more like a tale from a different aeon, but the lessons it teaches are timeless. It shows the power of the Bigger Fool Theory, which teaches you to pay too much for something in the belief that someone will come along and pay more. It illustrates the first law of business, which is that when you run out of money, you're dead. The dot.com bubble was a market in which, as sometimes happens, greed had outrun fear. Parties like that, as the Swedes would confirm, guarantee their own hangovers. (10 November 2001)

Where there's a tip

Those high-minded people at HSBC have tightened their rules about share tipping. From now on there will be as many 'sells' as 'buys' and the bank will put its money where its mouth is. This is a sore subject on Wall Street, where some of HSBC's opposite numbers tipped dot.com stocks at the top of the market and now find themselves being sued.

The HSBC two-tone scale will come as a shock, all the same, to old-fashioned brokers in London, who believe that their own graduated scale is far more sensitive, when fully understood. Thus, below 'buy' comes 'buy on weakness', which means 'don't buy', 'accumulate' (there is no market in the stock) and 'long-term hold' (we are brokers to the company). Then comes 'hold' (we can't remember why we bought them) and 'weak hold' (please hold them until we get out of them). 'Avoid' means 'going bust' and is rare. 'Sell' is rarer still. The analyst who acronymically wrote 'Can't Recommend A Purchase' about Robert Maxwell's shares got fired. Even 'buy' may mean 'we had lunch with these people and are hoping to impress them'. 'Fill your boots' means 'buy', but you should ask yourself who is filling them and what they may prove to contain. Where there's a tip, as the old maxim teaches, there's a tap. (8 September 2001)

A bad week for freedom, and I fear more casualties still to come
This was the week that included September 11, the day of the World Trade Center's destruction.

I would not care to live through such a week in the markets again, but others were denied the choice. The casualty lists from the World Trade Center are still coming in and a whole generation will be scarred by grief and loss. The survivors must pick themselves up and go on, and there is no arguing with the markets' first response, which is that the balance of the world's biggest economy, and all the other economies dependent on it, has been tilted, adversely. In our own economy, the confused signals which have been signalling boom and bust at once will now sort themselves out and turn red.

The central banks' response was to make money plentiful and make it cheaper. They were going by the book on damage limitation, though the Bank of England had trouble in finding the place. The damage that may count for most has been done to the markets themselves. It had almost come to seem natural for goods, services, money, capital, skills and people to move freely round the world to where they were needed, or wanted to go. Already that freedom had come up against a half-articulated resentment, expressed in the language of protest and violence. Now it has been challenged directly and with a violence never imagined. I fear that we shall see more casualties, economic, financial and human, before this is over. (22 September 2001)

Jam on the doughnuts – the new dispensation has winners as well as losers

What do you buy in a recession? Doughnuts? Well, someone must. Since 11 September the shares of Krispy Kreme Doughnuts have risen by 30 per cent, much to the joy of Tony Jackson at Charterhouse, who calls them 'an old favourite of ours', so I must be careful not to lunch there. Recessions are known to be good for sausage makers – people trade down from fillet steaks – and this may work for doughnuts, too. There are winners as well as losers in the new dispensation which began two months ago with the attack on the World Trade Center. Gas masks and anti-depressants have had a good run. Being handily placed for Afghanistan helps, so Thanksgiving has come early for Turkey, which need no longer worry about its finances.

Argentina, on the wrong side of the world, has been allowed to drift to the brink of default. Perhaps it should offer to swap its debts for the Falklands. When it offered this deal in the 1830s, the British refused, saying that these islands were ours already, but the file might be worth dusting off. The incongruous presence of Vladimir Putin as a guest on the Bush ranch in Texas signals that the big winner is Russia: in the right place, and producing more oil than Saudi Arabia, which is beginning to look like a loser. Oil has been a loser, too. Reduced production and weaker prices suggest that the market's immediate worry is that there will not be enough demand to go round. Either that, or the western world has learned how to run its cars on doughnuts. (17 November 2001)

Martyr or loser

Enron had a fan club to which I never belonged. So I missed out on its days of glory or notoriety and can catch up with it just in time for its collapse. This is or was a Texas-based power company with global ambitions – Wessex Water was one of its trophies – and when the new markets sprang up and allowed electricity to be traded, Enron took to them and dominated them. It was accused of oppressing the suffering peasants of California by making them pay the going rate for power or sit in the dark – one up, so the fan club thought, for market economics. Companies are always tempted to make extra money by playing the markets they trade in, like the cocoa market, in which Rowntree lost a fortune. Fancy accounting concealed Enron's losses but in the end the cash ran out, as it does. Irwin Stelzer, whose claim to be read is that he is thought to be one of Rupert Murdoch's vice-regents on earth, now puts Enron forward for canonisation as a martyred pioneer of free markets. It would be truer to say that those who live by the markets may perish by them. (8 December 2001)

The will to believe is what keeps markets going, until they go over the top

What a world-beating bezzle. It will go straight into the textbooks. Professors of economics will preach from it, to pupils who will have forgotten their lesson by the time the next bezzle comes round. That is the way it goes. Bezzles are cyclical. This one involves the $3.9 billion which was supposed to be in WorldCom's profits but, on a recount, turned out not to be.

Read all about bezzles in John Kenneth Galbraith's *The Great Crash*, his account of Wall Street's rise and precipitous fall in the 1920s. At any one time, says Galbraith, from the nation's banks and businesses, some money has gone walkies. The bezzle (his name for it) varies in size with the business cycle. In good times, when money seems to grow on trees, people can help themselves and get away with it. In bad times, trust dwindles, money is watched beadily and auditors are hawkish. The bezzle shrinks.

No one at WorldCom, so far as we know, put his hand in the till, or tucked money away in the offshore entities that were so favoured at Enron. Instead the profit and loss account was dressed up so as to sustain WorldCom's favourite graph of an ever-rising share price. That suited the managers who were rewarded with salaries and bonuses and options – but it suited everyone, from shareholders to sharepushers, for just as long as it lasted. This general will to believe is what swells the bezzle and what keeps stock markets going, until, in the end, it drives them over the top. (6 July 2002)

The stock market won't fall to zero, unless we've gone back to St Petersburg

The FTSE 100 index had fallen to below 3700 from a high of almost 7000 in December 1999.

Grrrrr. Not for 30 years has a bear market growled as fiercely as this one. In those distant days a friend of mine found himself questioned by a BBC interviewer with a lofty indifference to matters of finance. Why should it matter, he was asked, if the stock market went down? Because markets are forecasters, and if you believe them, hard times are ahead. Yes, yes, but was this just a fuss in the City? Ordinary people, surely, didn't own shares? Perhaps not, but their pension funds did. Well, then, had a stock market index ever gone to zero? Yes, said my friend, with assurance: St Petersburg, 1917.

Now, short of that precedent, the worst of the fall is presumably over. Leading shares have lost about half their value and are not likely to lose as much again, but the mood of the market is febrile. So many props for hope have been pulled out. Those who thought that each fall was a healthy correction, or strained to look across the valley to the heights beyond, or counted on some sort of consolidation which would clear the sellers out – all of them found new reasons for losing more money. Two months ago I saw markets as divided between optimists, who thought that things would soon get back to normal, and pessimists, who feared that this was so. Since then the pessimists seem to have gained ground, as the faith that the markets had placed in new economics and new technology comes to be seen as a classic aberration. From the South Sea Bubble onwards, stock markets have gone over the top at the end of long periods of genuine prosperity, when we are tempted to believe that life will always be like this, only more so. That was asking too much. (12 October 2002)

Spotting the gap

To everything there is a season, and this time last year I was looking for bargains in boredom. It would make a change, I thought. The stock market, in its exciting way, was going down like an express lift and the yield gap, after four decades of absence, was on its way back. Shares were once supposed to yield more than British government stocks, because they were thought to be riskier – they were issued by companies, which might default, whereas governments wouldn't. Then inflation came along to do governments' dirty work for them and the yield gap was turned inside out. Its return was a portent. It meant that by old-fashioned standards we could begin to look for value – starting with boring shares in solid companies which could be expected to plug on through good times and bad and carry on paying their dividends.

I picked out three shares that met this description, all of them yielding usefully more than government stocks did: Shell, Rio Tinto and Land Securities. A month later, the express lift jerked on its cable, stopped falling and bounced. By now two of my Boring Three have proved rewarding: Rio Tinto, up 20 per cent, and Land Secs, up 35 per cent.

Footnote on the yield gap: briefly sighted last year, it has receded into the darkness of space, like a comet. Leading shares now yield 3½ per cent, on average, and government stocks yield 4¾ per cent. They have lost value as the conviction has dawned that Gordon Brown will need to issue more and more of them. If inflation were really as low as he says it is, they would look cheap, but the markets don't believe him, and no wonder. (14 February 2004)

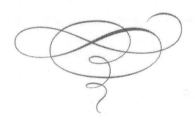

Shell explodes

A new entry for my Bad Investment Guide. Last year I was looking for boring shares in solid companies which could be expected to plug on through bad times and good: 'If there are bargains, this is where to find them.' So it was, but I should not have been so sure of Shell. After decades of elevating boredom into a corporate art form, Shell is displacing the Beckhams from the headlines, with its reserves and directors evaporating in a cloud of embarrassing e-mails: 'This is absolute dynamite and must be destroyed.' It wasn't, of course. Experience suggests that e-mails never are. I suppose the culprits will plead that they were only trying to spare us excitement. Well, thanks. (24 April 2004)

"It remains for me to thank Kleinwort Benson for its investment advice, well timed for the season of excess. 'Remain seriously overweight in the United Kingdom.' Thanks chaps, I wasn't thinking of moving. **"**

CHAPTER TWO

CURRENCY COCKTAILS

How do you like your money – shaken, stirred or with a twist?

Rigging markets is illegal, except when governments do it, and British governments were and are constantly tempted to rig the market in sterling. They briefly succeeded in tying the pound into Europe's Exchange Rate Mechanism, and there is always the prospect of folding it into Europe's single currency. I was the ERM's lonely opponent. Received opinion was all for it, and all three political parties tied their fortunes to the ERM, at an election which the Conservatives had the misfortune to win. Five months later the pound was thrown out, ignominiously and expensively but much to our advantage. Memories of this debacle must have helped to keep us out of the euro and to make martinis – and negronis, too – affordable. I keep an eye on them.

Sterling sets sail across the Channel with the gangways down

The UK joins the European Exchange Rate Mechanism.

We have embarked on an attempt to rig the biggest market of all, the foreign exchanges. We must then try to make our economy fit our exchange rate. We are told that this is an essential discipline, or an alternative – as if there were one – to self-discipline. Some people even expect to enjoy it. Already the first and airiest expectations have dispersed. Markets live by anticipation, and this marriage had, in the modern style, been thoroughly anticipated – honeymoon first, wedlock afterwards. Only the naïve could see it as a white wedding with a happy electoral event due nine months later.

Are we doomed to go into these arrangements at the wrong rate – too high in 1926, when Churchill put us back on the gold standard, too low in 1949, when Stafford Cripps devalued? Harold Wincott thought so, a quarter of a century ago, watching the Wilson government impaling itself on a $2.80 parity for sterling; but Wincott wondered whether there was, or could long remain, such a thing as a right rate. An exchange rate, he thought, was a price – and prices change.

Keynes thought so, too. The Bretton Woods system, his legacy to the post-war world, was meant to provide for that. Exchange rates would be fixed, within narrow limits, until it was time for a change – which the country concerned would agree with the IMF. Alas, it did not work like that. Exchange rates were locked into place, defended at high cost, and changed only in a series of violent jerks and successive crises which in the end brought down the system.

We have heard much about what the ERM can do for us. Let me say once more that the ERM can do nothing for us that we could not, if we chose, do for ourselves. Our partners in the ERM will not keep sterling within its bounds. That is our responsibility. The ERM gives us no new weapons. In or out, we have only three of them: intervening in the markets, changing interest rates, or changing fiscal policy – crisis packages or mini-budgets, as they used to be called in their unlamented day. Being in the ERM will not bring down our inflation by any means which were not available to us outside it. To rely on the ERM as an external discipline is to say that we either cannot or will not manage our affairs and would prefer that others acted for us. They will, of course, act for themselves.

Churchill came to bemoan his return to the gold standard (and to blame his advisers), but at the time he was a convert. 'Nations on the gold standard,' he said, 'are like ships whose gangways are joined together.' No one cared to tell him that ships whose gangways are joined together are singularly ill equipped to sail the seas. What gangways are good for is boarding. (13 October 1990)

Onwards and upwards to my goal – the $2 martini

I live in hope of the $2 martini. As the exchange rate inches up towards the magic figure of $2 = £1, I yearn to fly westwards towards some reliable source of martinis (the Ritz-Carlton, Boston offers a choice of 16) and mop them up while the illusion lasts. Now, with the pound nine-tenths of the way there, the terms of the trade are well in my favour and it seems foolish to wait.

I am of course the beneficiary of two central banks, one here and one in Germany. The Bundesbank, from which we choose to take our tune, is sitting on its policy of dear money. The United States Federal Reserve has no such inhibitions. It has had a sick banking system to nurse, the money supply has been looking decidedly pinched, and cheap money is the prescribed treatment for both. Low interest rates have driven investors away from the money market and sent them back into stocks – though not yet into property. The Dow-Jones index has been defying gravity, and Nicholas Brady, the President's amiable millionaire friend who is Secretary of the Treasury, contrives to look cheerful, except when he sees the polls. At intervals he presses the Japanese to make their currency more expensive – and martinis, in yen terms, even cheaper.

I have from time to time wondered what would have happened if we had linked the pound's exchange rate not to the mark, as we

have, but to the dollar, as we always used to. Three plain consequences stand out: our money rates would be much lower, we
should be further out of recession, and I should be left sucking the
gin out of an olive. (13 June 1992)

Happy hour

My martini exchange rate target is on the horizon. This
week the pound touched $1.90 – only another 10 cents
before we fly to America, there to absorb ourselves in martinis or
vice versa, until the foreign exchanges wake up and see sense. To
compare what money will buy, in London and New York, is to see
that a one-for-one exchange rate – £1 = $1 – would be more like
it. Today's exchange rate must make British goods and services
(martinis, for example) uncompetitive against those of the world's
largest economy.

The markets, though, fret about sterling's weakness – oh dear,
we have lost ground to the mark, we are at the bottom of the
European league table again... We are mesmerised by the mark,
just as we used, with more reason, to be fixated on the dollar.
Germany's problems remain the opposite of ours. The Bundesbank
complains that its money supply is still growing too strongly – so
no interest rate cuts until it starts to behave. The US Federal
Reserve is being nudged to lower its rates and keep the fitful US
recovery going. The pull of interest rates hoists the mark, lowers
the dollar, and leaves the pound with the worst of both worlds. It
is not a great way to manage a currency or an economy, and I
wonder how long we can subsist on a policy of hanging on and
hoping. (4 July 1992)

Martini time – it's my moment of madness and Lamont's unhappy hour

The two-dollar martini has brushed against my lips like an
angel's kiss. At teatime on Monday the magic figure flashed
up on the screen: £1 = $2. It was my signal to fly the Atlantic and
lap up martinis while such a mad exchange rate lasted – but it
lasted no more than a moment, to leave the pound bobbing

tantalisingly at $1.99. Judging by this week's trade figures, others can hear the siren call. A surge in imports, at a time of deep recession and flat demand, tells its own story.

If there is one thing madder than a two-dollar exchange rate for sterling, it is the idea that the rate needs to be bolstered by dearer money. That was the spectre confronting Norman Lamont on his return from Tuscany. If only he had yielded to temptation and stayed on to make his own olive oil! Now (so he must be musing) all his home thoughts from abroad are coming true, all the things that could go wrong have started to happen – in Frankfurt the squareheads won't budge, in Paris the polls are running against Maastricht and in London, if he hasn't got an old-fashioned sterling crisis, he is quite close enough for discomfort. He is under pressure to raise interest rates, when every indicator he has and every spark of common sense must tell him what the stock market is telling him – that it would be the quick way to make matters worse. Debt and dear money got us into recession and have kept us there, falsifying every Treasury forecast and blighting every hope.

Now what? The Chancellor must try to stick it out for three weeks. Then the French vote on Maastricht will be relayed to the world's finance ministers, who (as it happens) will all be in Washington for the International Monetary Fund meeting. A 'Non' vote would test Europe's exchange rates and might easily blow them apart. Mr Lamont would find himself in a poker game, playing for high stakes with moderate cards and not too many chips. He has gone out of his way to promise that, whatever other countries may do with their currencies, he will not budge on sterling – bound by hoops of steel to the mark at DM2.95 and now set against the dollar at an incredible $2. How he must wish he had taken my advice, tying sterling to the dollar and not to the mark, relishing dollar-based interest rates of 3 or 4 per cent! He is committed, though, and I take him to have made this a resigning matter. It is 25 years since a Chancellor went down with his currency.

(9 August 1992)

Expletive deleted – after the $2 martini, here comes the negroni crisis

The man who got it right was Richard M. Nixon. When he was President, and the world's currencies were (as now) in turmoil, the chairman of the Federal Reserve was concerned that the market's pressures would (as now) find a focus in Italy, destabilising the lira. He told the White House and the White House told the Oval Office. Mr Nixon rose to the occasion. 'I don't,' he replied, 'give a [expletive deleted] about the lira.' His verdict was recorded on tape and emerged in the Watergate hearings, scandalising William Rees-Mogg, who as editor of *The Times* thought that this was no way to talk on so serious a topic. It was and is just the way to talk. The Italians have been heading the rush towards monetary union, believing that when the day comes their financial troubles will be over. Officials in the Finance Ministry and the Banca d'Italia favour it, arguing that anything would be better than having to work for Italian politicians.

The bill for all these simplistic assumptions has now started to come in. It worries other members of the European Exchange Rate Mechanism, who fear that if the Italian wheel comes off their whole conveyance may collapse. (The Finns, who were semi-detached, have come off already.) The danger is of digging in to defend the indefensible. Direct observation suggests that at these exchange rates a negroni is as overpriced in Florence as a martini is cheap in New York. What rocked the lira in Richard Nixon's day was Britain's decision to float the pound, justified by a Conservative Chancellor. Experience showed (he said) that a country should not wait too long to change an exchange rate, if balance of payments trends were adverse and the exchange rate came under pressure. (12 September 1992)

With a twist

My quest for the two-dollar martini has been foiled, and I fear we shall never see $2 = £1 again. Even so, having bought my dollars before leaving, I was able to enjoy a $1.95 martini at the Metropolitan Club in Washington when the rate in the world outside was $1.71. Nectar. (3 October 1992)

Straight up

The martini exchange rate, round about $1.60, is off the top but still represents good value. I was checking on it in New York last month when Alan Greenspan of the Federal Reserve let the markets know that interest rates could go down as well as up. They took him to mean that the exchange rate could go down as well as down. General turmoil followed. Eddie George (showing Mr Greenspan how to do it) says that the pound has been looking wobbly but he hopes it will soon perk up. Martini fanciers hope so, too. (18 March 1995)

Taste that kir

One more heave towards the ten-franc kir. The banks still quote you 9.3 francs to the pound, but Le Touquet's shopkeepers, I find, will round it up to 10. Like everybody else in France, they need the trade. My advice is sinking in: *votez non*, *votez souvent*, I told the French people, and they voted 'Non' to poor, hairless, harassed Alain Juppé, who always seems to me to have escaped from a black-and-white sitcom and can now go back there. Another such vote this weekend and the franc should be weak enough to make the kir affordable. If it derailed the single currency, that, too, would be helpful. (31 May 1997)

Let us raise our glasses to the ten-franc kir while we still have the chance

This is a proud moment for me. The ten-franc kir has come. All last week the rate of exchange was pushing fiercely upwards, on Monday it faltered but rallied, the French franc closed at 9.9995 to the pound, and on Tuesday morning, bingo! It hit 10.01. So my long campaign in these columns has paid off, just in time for the annual exodus to the Dordogne. My influence on France's recent election — *votez non*, *votez souvent*, I urged, when the franc was at 9.45 — may well have been decisive. As that first cooling kir comes to your zinc-topped table, raise your glass to the column that made it affordable. It is too much to expect the Confederation of British Industry to join us. The pound will be getting too hot for it. Any minute now, in its oxymoronic way, the CBI will call for an exchange rate that is stable but competitive.

I would rather argue that a rate of exchange is a price in a market, that prices in markets move about, and that attempts to rig them are counterproductive and doomed to disappointment. France is caught up in an elaborate attempt to rig the currency markets of Europe, though its new government jibs at the price that has had to be paid and would have to be paid from now on. No wonder some of the shine has come off the French franc, and off the shiny single currency that it was meant to join, once the market was suitably rigged.

The pound plays no part in these manoeuvres, or not yet. That is one reason why it is popular. A solid record of sound monetary management would have been a better reason, but we cannot claim that, or not yet. This week's figures show that inflation is on its way up again. My advice to readers is to pour those ten-franc kirs down while our victory lasts. (12 July 1997)

Cheaper in Biarritz

Now that the French have given up on the ten-franc kir, I suppose that I must follow their example. This will placate those readers who have patiently explained to me that what I meant was a kir that, if it cost ten francs, could be bought by a visiting Brit for a pound. Thinking, last week, that it might still be holding out in France's furthest corners, I went to look for it in Biarritz and had my enterprise rewarded when I came across the hundred-franc Scotch. This is the shop price for a respectable bottle of blended Scotch whisky, which, if the rate of exchange gets no worse, will now be cheaper in Biarritz than in the duty-free shops at Heathrow. They have been warning their customers that in two years' time travellers within Europe will lose this concession. Stand up for it, they say, write to your MP about it. A Euro conference in its defence is scheduled for next month in Brussels: buy a bottle and bring it along.

I am unsympathetic. Providing access to aircraft is no more than a tiresome necessity for airports. They earn their corn as shopping malls with captive customers, imprisoned for hours on end. It is hard to say that they deserve a special deal from the excisemen or the Chancellor. He would do better to follow Kenneth Clarke's example and bring the price of Scotch in its country of origin closer to the price of Scotch in Biarritz. (30 August 1997)

Alice comes to Euroland, where everybody wins

When Alice fell down the rabbit hole and into Wonderland, she found herself in a pool of tears. A duck and a dodo were swimming about in it, along with several other curious creatures. She led them to shore, but they had to get dry and the Dodo suggested a Caucus Race. It set out a circular course and they ran round for half an hour or so until the Dodo announced that the race was over. Then they asked who had won, and this left the Dodo thinking deeply. At last it proclaimed, 'Everybody has won, and all must have prizes.'

In the Euro Caucus Race, the Dodo is an Emu. All of its flock have been running round in circles, pretending to dry their economies out, and this week brings the long-awaited result. Which of them has qualified for the great Euro prize? Who can join the single currency and look forward to economic and monetary union? To nobody's surprise, the Emu has proclaimed, 'They all can.'

Everybody has won, all have qualified and in the first week in May all will come and claim their prizes. Alice might think that this was a comical race and an odd way of deciding things, that no handicap could bring this ill-assorted field of ducks and drakes together, and that the result was a fix. The Emu would call it a vision. Now she must expect them to crowd round her, calling out in a confused way 'Prizes! Prizes!' By the time she has handed out something to everyone, her pockets will be empty, except for a thimble. 'Hand it over,' the Emu will say, before giving it back, adding that this is a concession and will be subject to review. Of one thing Alice can be certain: the Emu's Caucus Race will end where it began, in tears.

One of the more curious entries in this race is the lira, which has just set a new record: all hail to the 3000-lire negroni! I shall raise a glass to it in the Bar Giacosa, in Florence, where Count Negroni first composed the drink that has endeared his memory to us all. It is true that 3000 lire will not buy me a very large negroni, or much more than a plate of crisps, but the rate of exchange is what matters and it has gone charging upwards through the 3000 level for the first time that I can remember. I have never shared the robust indifference of Richard Nixon, who could not give a deleted expletive about the lira. It was the lira's collapse that put sterling in the firing line and shot us out of the Exchange Rate Mechanism. It was an Italian prime minister and finance minister – one of them now charged with complicity to murder, the other sent to prison for corruption – who ambushed Margaret Thatcher at the Rome summit and committed Europe to a timetable for monetary union. Italy has been preparing for it on the health farm principle: diet now, cheat a little, binge afterwards. If it came to the point, the Emu might have trouble digesting the lira. (28 March 1998)

Make Tokyo cheap

Venturing into Fortnum & Mason, I find myself charged by a phalanx of Japanese shoppers. They are worthy of their martial ancestors and the weakness of their currency does not seem to be putting them off. I would be astonished to learn that British shoppers are roaming the Ginza, using their strong pounds to snap up bargains. When I was last in Japan, my host recommended me to think of my 10,000-yen notes as whisky tokens. 'Don't try to work out what they're worth,' he said. 'It will only upset you.' By western standards Tokyo is still amazingly expensive, and by Japanese standards London is still cheap.

Last week the Americans came riding ostentatiously to the yen's rescue, but that looked to me like a propitiatory gesture, ahead of the President's visit to Beijing. The Chinese have been voicing their fear that the yen's fall will set their own currency sliding. I notice that Nikko, the Tokyo-based broker, thinks the yen still has further to fall. Struggling to kick-start their sluggish economy, the Japanese need to bring the eager shoppers back from Fortnum's to the Ginza. A cheaper yen strikes me as the obvious way to do that. (27 June 1998)

Don't mention the **r*

The single European currency formally came into existence on 1 January 1999, although euro notes and coins did not come into circulation until 1 January 2002.

As a gesture of peace and goodwill, I have declared this week's column a safe zone in which a notorious four-letter word will not appear. There will be enough of it everywhere else. You will not read here about a new synthetic currency, lumbering to its birth in Europe as the old year dies. To learn how to change other currencies into it and back again through a process called triangulation, or to admire the City's efforts to prepare for it, you must retrieve the *Financial Times's* supplement from the bathroom floor or the cat's litter tray. Inquiries about travellers' cheques to take on holiday should be directed to your bank, though all you will need is a credit card that works in holes in the wall.

Or you could go to Switzerland, which will always take genuine money and is rightly happy with the currency it has. I have long thought that if we must merge the pound, we should merge it with the Swiss franc. Indeed, as a step towards ever closer union, I am applying to the authorities in Berne for the City to be recognised as an additional canton of Switzerland. Dafter ideas are being wished on us and on Europe, but for this week this column is free of them. (19/26 December 1998)

Europe's new currency becomes a euro-dollar and the markets hedge their bets

After the ten-franc kir, the euro-dollar. Europe's unhappy new currency has slid so far and fast that one euro is scarcely worth more than one dollar, and at any moment now they may become a straight swap: $1 = €1. Some visionary is then sure to urge that the two of them should be locked together forever, at parity, as the first step towards a single currency for the whole world. It would be a cause worthy of Sir Samuel Brittan and his readers will look forward to a weighty column, to be erected in the *Financial Times*'s rolling parkland as soon as the occasion offers. I would simply say that locking currencies together has not worked very well so far. It has made the euro a metaphysical currency, in the sense that Dr Johnson coined for metaphysical poetry: 'The most heterogeneous ideas are yoked by violence together.'

Yoking the pound to the euro no longer looks the sure thing that its backers said it was. They encouraged businessmen to think that we should be joining the single currency, like it or not, so why argue? The markets have been reassessing that bet and hedging it. In mergers, prices talk. If this merger was on course to happen as soon as the next election was out of the way, the price of British government stock would be converging with the prices of government stocks on the Continent. Not a bit of it. They have been moving in opposite directions. The only convergence now going on is the steady drift down to the one-dollar euro. (17 July 1999)

Charity at parity

'Don't let's be beastly to the euro! Don't let's be beastly to the mon: we'll watch it sink to parity And look on it with charity. . .' Words and music by Noel Coward, suitably adapted. Mon = money, and rhymes with bun, or whatever.

Poor old single currency. Its best friends are the British skiers who can now afford resorts that have been closed to them for years. Its supporters at Britain in Europe are engaged on their umpteenth relaunch. The Foreign Office, always whistling to keep other people's spirits up, explains what a success the euro is, and the Treasury audibly doesn't. No doubt Gordon Brown's switch out of gold into euros, one of last year's least successful investment decisions, has soured him. This week the euro sank lower than ever against the pound and dipped below parity with the dollar. In a true spirit of not being beastly I now offer my confident prediction for this currency: if it lasts long enough, it will bounce. Currencies do. Even the rouble has its moments. (29 January 2000)

Currency cocktail

My fact-finding visit to Italy established that the negroni exchange rate remains highly favourable. You can still get three of these excellent drinks for 30,000 lire, which leaves you change out of a tenner, and two of them are quite enough to get you going. The rate is a function of the euro, which is going through another of its sticky patches. This has to be somebody's fault and the blame has been awarded to Wim Duisenberg, the mop-headed Dutchman who governs the European Central Bank. He is under attack from all sides for not cutting interest rates. This, he is told, should be his contribution to keeping Europe's economy going, and everyone else's economy, too. He thinks that his job is to keep inflation down, and that after the euro's loss of value there is quite a lot of it about. These are the priorities of an old-fashioned central banker. If he goes on like this (and if the French do not contrive to get rid of him) he may begin to make his currency sound credible. Bad news for negroni drinkers, of course. (5 May 2001)

Short change

I shall miss the ten-franc kir and the 3000-lire negroni. They were among the euro's more solid or liquid achievements, for its weakness has enabled me to drink on favourable terms in all my preferred destinations in Europe, except, of course, Switzerland, which has kept its nerve and its currency. I found that in Siena a tenner would buy three negronis but that after two I lost control of the experiment. Now we shall all have to adapt to the new currency cocktail and to work out whether, if £1 = €1.6245, we are being short-changed by the barman. I expect so, but more research is sure to be needed. (5 January 2002)

An olive ahead

There seems to be life after death for the ten-franc kir. A cherished cause of mine, this represented the rate of exchange (£1 = FF10) at which it became economical to drink in France. When the franc went the ten-franc kir went with it, and since then the euro has been creeping upwards, but even so the

€1.56 which your pound will now buy are equivalent to FF10.25, which leaves you an olive ahead of the game. Unless, that is, your bar has predictably taken advantage of the currency conversion to round prices up.

France has a new finance minister called Francis Mer who thinks that the euro has already risen too far. He would like to see it, so he says, not necessarily strong but solid. He must have learned his economics, such as they are, at the CBI, which always says that it wants the pound to be stable but competitive. This is like wanting girls to be prim but improper. (22 June 2002)

On the •

THE Dalmatian coast is still a euro-free zone and I have been enjoying the ten-cuna Prosec. (This week's rate: £1 = 11.44 Croatian cunas.) All the same, I think the Croats missed a trick when they split their currency off from the Yugoslav dinar. They should have standardised on the spot, which would have had its own symbol and, of course, its spot rate of exchange. We could all understand 100 • = 1 Dalmatian and 101 Dalmatians = 1 Croat, or Coat. (22 June 2002)

If you don't like a strong pound, try a weak one, or switch from kirs to martinis

HUng be the heavens with black; yield, day, to night. Cancel that skiing holiday now. The ten-franc kir has sunk out of sight and who can say when it will surface again?

The dollar has fallen from grace, the euro has benefited and the pound has been caught in the crossfire. We shall all have some adjusting to do, starting with the European Commission, which complains that the eurozone cannot even compete as things are. The new guard at the top of the Bank of England and the Treasury may have to learn what the old guard could tell them – that the problems of a strong currency are nothing to the problems of a weak one. The rest of us may have to go to New York, where the pound is at its highest for three years. Onwards and upwards to the two-dollar martini! (18 January 2003)

Civilised currencies

'The only way to judge a government,' wrote my lamented colleague Auberon Waugh, 'is by the pound's rate of exchange against the few civilised currencies that matter: the French franc, the Italian lira and the Thai baht.' At 12 francs to the pound, Mrs Thatcher's first government had done well and he would vote for her. Against the lira, Mr Blair's first government did even better, achieving a negroni index equivalent to 3300 lire to the pound, a record. Suddenly, though, the pound is sinking faster than Venice and the index is down below 2800. Can this be a last-minute attempt to pass the famous five tests? I may have to look into comparative purchasing power in Harry's Bar. More research is needed and, of course, more public funding. (10 May 2003)

Negroni, Berlusconi?

The resourceful Silvio Berlusconi plans to give Italy a top tax rate of 33 per cent, which would be the lowest in Europe. This, he hopes, will encourage his countrymen to break the habits of their lifetimes and submit to paying taxes. If they did, Italy might fit into the Stability and Growth Pact without too much creative accounting, but if not, its public finances (and the Pact) will be even more precarious. Where will this leave the negroni index, always my benchmark?

My inquiries sent me to Rome, where I could update my negroni index (still refreshing and affordable) and my knowledge of Berlusconomics. The test case of the moment is Alitalia, the cash-guzzling national airline, which greeted my arrival by going out on strike and brought the Roman taxi drivers out in sympathy. The Berlusconi government's response was to tell Alitalia to economise on directors.

The historian Livy tells us that, back in the days of the Roman Republic, the official flute players went on strike because they had been refused their traditional banquet on the Capitol, downing flutes and walking out as far as Tivoli. The Senate persuaded their hosts there to give them a banquet, at which they passed out, waking up to find that they had been carted back to the Forum. Mr Berlusconi might usefully try this. (24 April/15 May 2004)

CHAPTER THREE

THE GOOD, THE BAD AND THE UGLY

Heroes and villains of the financial world, from the Queen Mother to Robert Maxwell

Singular characters lurk beneath the City's sober uniforms. All human life is there, as *The People*, always a good read on Sunday mornings, used to claim for itself. When Polly Peck – the company built up by the now fugitive Asil Nadir – ran out of money and credibility, the expensive furniture in its Berkeley Square office was put up for sale and I went along to the preview. 'What would be an appropriate car,' I was asked, 'in a company of this kind, for the chairman's girlfriend?' I demurred. 'What about a top-of-the-range BMW?' I agreed. 'Well, what would you say to 14 of them?' I had no answer to that, but let me introduce you to some of the rest of the cast.

Rope trick

Signor Calvi, the president of Banco Ambrosiano, was found hanging under Blackfriars Bridge in London in 1982. Signor Sindona's enemies arranged for him to be poisoned in his Italian jail cell.

The bank loan of the week involves Michele Sindona – 'God's banker' before Roberto Calvi took over the account. Sindona is being lent by the New York jail where he is serving 25 years for the Franklin National fraud, to face trial back home in Italy. He should read the small print. The prospect of giving evidence in an Italian court is not always healthy. Calvi got no further than Blackfriars Bridge and an odder fate overtook a lieutenant of Sindona's, who was also to be extradited to Italy to give evidence. He tried to escape from his American prison by climbing down a rope. It broke, and his cellmate, a fat Colombian drug smuggler, landed on top of him and squashed him flat. Query: who supplied him with the rope? (29 September 1984)

J.J. carries his bat

A deafening City send-off this week for John – always J.J. – Warr. For 35 years a pillar of the money market (first with Union Discount, then with Clive, as deputy chairman) he is giving himself the time he needs as president-elect of the MCC. Fast bowler for Cambridge, Middlesex, England and the discount houses in their annual festive match against the Stock Exchange, well-informed observer of markets from Lombard Street to Tattersalls, disciplinary steward of the Jockey Club, the City's most prized and funniest speaker, he leaves the place looking, in his absence, distinctly ordinary.

In a class of its own among the J.J. stories is that of his Binney Award, for civilian gallantry. Armed robbers escaping from a City bank ran down an alleyway off Cornhill – and straight into the top-hatted figure of J.J. on his money market round, looking about nine feet high and broad in proportion, blocking the way, refusing to budge. They threatened him. Finally, at close range, they fired at him. He felt nothing, but later found that his suit appeared to be dotted with moth holes. They were powder burns. By a mercy, the cartridge had contained powder but no shot. He was then asked what he had done when the raiders fired. 'At this point,' said J.J., 'I decided to play for a draw.' (18 July 1987)

King Richard

A leonine roar was the first I heard of Dick Wilkins. I was being towed around by the gentle Donald Constant of *The Times* who, putting his head round the door of the partners' room at Wedd's, would be greeted fortissimo with 'Aha! It's John the Baptist!' The senior partner was robust and rotund – he peaked at 23 stone – with the strong nerve and swift reaction which he had brought to racing his power boats or tearing round Brooklands in his Ferrari. Cars were a passion of his, steeplechasing was another, and the story is that he was driving back from Cheltenham with the Queen Mother when the Rolls-Royce sputtered to a halt. 'Perhaps, Dick,' said his royal passenger, 'we should have come in one of your other Rollers?'

He dominated the stock markets – merging his firm, the leading jobbers in Government stock, with Durlachers, the leaders in shares, and himself leading by example and from the front. No one could be ruder to the great or kinder to the lowly. In retirement he roosted at the Savoy (he was a director, and they understood his frustrating diet) – snorting at events and missing the excitement. The market floor which he ruled has gone, and now Dick has gone too! No one will ever thus dominate the new, dispersed, electronic markets; King Richard was the last of his line. (18 February 1989)

Tip for Tiny

The inspectors into House of Fraser find a striking phrase for Tiny Rowland. They describe him as his own worst enemy. Well, now – the field must be a large one, the event competitive, the Fayeds would be fancied and Mr Rowland would carry top weight, but for all that I think my money would be on him. I wonder if the inspectors have any other tips as good. (17 March 1990)

Polly's folly

Polly Peck was a conglomerate controlled by Asil Nadir, a Turkish Cypriot entre-
preneur who made his first fortune in fruit packing; it was one of the hottest stocks
of the 1980s boom, but Nadir fled back to Cyprus in 1990 to avoid fraud charges.

Everything must go from 42 Berkeley Square, where Polly
Peck set up its head office, regardless of cost or taste. The
house is crammed from cellar to roof with lavish purchases – gilt-
wood torchères in the boardroom, gross chandeliers, wall-to-wall
tapestries, a Turner or two, and period furniture from the stately
dealers of Bond Street which must soon be on its way back. The
auction is at Phillips on Tuesday. Polly's palazzo bears out one of
the oldest rules of all: building an ostentatious head office is a sure
sign of trouble in store. Professor Parkinson applied this to New
Delhi and St Peter's. I would add Lloyd's of London, Commercial
Union, P & O and, I expect, the £60 million pad now on order for
Sir Richard Attenborough as chairman of Channel 4.

I found my first and last visit oppressive, but if you like the
Polly style, go along to the sale – and see whether the dealers will
maintain, as buyers, the fabulous prices they got when they were
selling. Polly assets held out of this sale include a small fleet of
BMW cars. These were provided for the use of 14 ladies who seem
to have been consultants. The cars have been called back. I do not
know what has happened to the ladies. (16 February 1991)

Freedom from Maxwell – cheap at the price of a case of Bollinger

The Lady Ghislaine was Maxwell's yacht, from which he fell, jumped or was pushed.

It was late and I was, as I thought, alone in the industrial slum
which then served the *Daily Telegraph* as a City Office, when
I became aware of a vast, looming presence behind me. I turned
round to find Robert Maxwell. Heaven preserve us, I thought, he's
bought the paper. This is the end. After a lifetime of being careful
not to work for him, I was trapped. What I said was: 'Hello, Mr
Maxwell, how nice to see you, what can I do for you?' 'Ah,
Christopher, I am looking for the party? Where is the party?' I
knew of no party, but suggested that, since I had a case of

champagne by my left foot, we could have one of our own. He was tempted, but stumped off to seek his hosts in a more salubrious part of the building.

I would have enjoyed our private party, and at a dozen of Bollinger I would have got off lightly. Think of all the people who turned round to find that Maxwell had bought the companies they worked for – and, with the companies, control of their pension funds. They were sheep to be shorn. They had no choice in the matter. Belonging to the pension fund might well have been a condition of service.

We now see ministers engaged in the familiar tactic of passing the blame to the City, where they are promoting a whip-round. The long ears of security were picking up signals from the *Lady Ghislaine* – but then, the Funnies' file on Maxwell must run into volumes and go back to 1945. Nor can I think it contains anything to surprise the Bank of England, which at least prevented him from buying a bank – not, I may say, for want of trying. He already owned a company which printed cheque books, and would doubtless have overprinted them all in his favour. (20 June 1991)

The Bank of Cocaine and Colombia adds a new terror to recession

Hands up anyone who thought there wasn't a fraud at the Bank of Credit and Commerce International (Manuel Noriega?). It was the world's most bizarre bank, its two middle initials were said to stand for Cocaine and Colombia, and its collapse is more shocking than surprising – but is just what the economy does not need.

I warned six months ago that the credit squeeze and freeze would serve to dry up the ordinary flows of cash through the economy. The casualties of drought, I said, would follow. So they have – businesses are dying for want of payments. Now comes our biggest bank failure for many years, and thousands of sole traders and small businesses, and some not so small, have had their cheque books frozen – along with £250 million of their money. Savings and their managers sometimes melt away, the 'fringe banks' of 20 years ago disappeared in a puff of malodorous smoke, but we are not used to seeing bank doors close on the working capital of ordinary businesses.

The failure of a bank, and for that matter the exposure of a fraud, are classic symptoms of the contraction of credit. They make it worse, as the BCCI affair shows. It is not all the fault of some unnamed group of kite flyers and book fiddlers. It is part and parcel of a financially driven recession, compounded by the Treasury, which did not understand what would happen when companies and people and (finally) banks ran out of money. (13 July 1991)

K.C.O.B.E.

I am delighted to learn that the City's senior banker has been honoured for his services. He is not, as you might think, some aging Baring or supernumerary Barclay. Kung Chao Wu, 'K.C.' to all, who becomes an honorary Officer of the Order of the British Empire, has been the Bank of China's man in London since 1944. He is the first port of call for anyone in the City with a Chinese puzzle and his network is unique. 'K.C. knows everybody,' as Robin Leigh-Pemberton put it, 'and everyone knows K.C.' That was at the City party to mark K.C.'s half-century in banking with the presentation of a silver dish. He answered in style – 'You and I, Mr Governor, we are survivors' – and then picked up the dish, peered at the hallmark and affected a double-take: 'Made in Taiwan?' (21 September 1991)

Currant in the cake

I am saddened by the death of Sir Patrick Meaney, least portentous of boardroom knights and most ebullient. He had got to the top without pull – chairman of Rank, director of Imperial Chemical Industries, deputy chairman and occasional power broker at the Midland Bank – and he stayed there without pomposity. At Thomas Tilling, where he made his name, he took over a company chaired by my father, a deal which left both sides content. 'I liked doing business with him,' Meaney told me, years later. 'He knew what few people know, that you always leave a currant in the other fellow's slice of cake.' When BTR bid for Tilling, Meaney proved a debonair fighter. I was at the Tilling shareholders' meeting when an anxious old lady asked who these BTR people were who kept sending all these papers to her – what, she wanted to know, did BTR stand for? Pat Meaney bounced to his feet: 'Bust Tilling and Run!' (25 July 1992)

Getting into the papers

The chairman of the Press Complaints Committee had accused Princess Diana of manipulating the press.

I have never been manipulated by the Princess of Wales but I hope that if I were I should behave like a gentleman. To others the experience seems to have come as a shock, unless, as I dare say, they have been acting out a fantasy. I am less easily shocked. Even the notion that the spirited publicist Brian Basham might seek to influence me on Lord King's behalf was one that I could face with equanimity. He is in the business, after all. Now that British Airways has subjected him to the usual fate of messengers and shot him, I urge him to join forces with the Princess, under the slogan 'For King and country'. I am not worried about people who want to get things into the papers. The people who want to keep things out worry me. (23 January 1993)

A draft on memory

Sir Jeremy Morse leaves Lloyds Bank on a high note. The results, out this week, for his last year as chairman will put Lloyds at the top of the Big Four, for the second year running. I shall miss that formidable and deeply stocked mind. I think of him at the party he gave in the bank for the centenary of T. S. Eliot. Like Sir Jeremy, Eliot welcomed the routine of banking and was working for Lloyds in Cornhill when he wrote 'The Waste Land', with its haunting images drawn from the City. Sir Jeremy began to read from it:

A crowd flowed over London Bridge, so many,
I had not thought death had undone so many...

He checked for a moment and continued, and I thought, hearing him, that there was something not quite familiar about his text. Was this a draft rediscovered in Lloyds' archives? No – but Eliot's words had moved Sir Jeremy to tears, so that he could not see through his glasses. He had finished the poem from memory. (13 February 1993)

Supergnome

I am taking out a short position in George Soros. To me, he looks overbought and overdone. I do not grudge him his profit from selling sterling on Black Wednesday – even the Treasury now admits that the collapse of its policy is what has got the economy going – but it has made him out to be a Supergnome, who by his dealings has the power to raise a currency or bring it down.

Some loudmouth in Washington wants Mr Soros investigated, to see if Mr Soros has been rigging the foreign exchanges. I can acquit him. A billion-dollar deal could scarcely rig a market which turns over $1000 billion on an ordinary day – and Black Wednesday was not that. The people who seriously tried to rig the markets were the central bankers, and much good it did them. Now, though, the Supergnome is constantly pronouncing on the future of the mark or the franc, and dealers find that their rumours spread better if they put his name in front of them. Such pronouncements and rumours can be self-fulfilling, for a while. Then the marketplace finds a new idol. Robert Maxwell put it about that he had moved into cash before Wall Street's Black Monday. (31 July 1993)

Courage and style

I first met Jocelyn Hambro (who died at the weekend) when he gave Hambros' first press conference. Thirty years ago that was a dashing thing for a family merchant bank to do, but here was the new sixth-generation chairman, showing us around the balance sheet as if it were his garden: 'Unit trusts? Yes, we're going to start some. Why? Well, first of all, to improve our placing power. Government stocks? We've got rid of them. I don't know what you think of the present Prime Minister – I think he's the worst since Lord North...'

That annoyed Harold Wilson's government into having Hambros investigated, but backing his judgement was part of the chairman's job. It had set him selling MG cars to Texans, who had not until then (so they told him) seen a malted milk machine with wheels on. It encouraged him to put £1 million of the bank's money on Mark Weinberg's ideas about life assurance – a bet that paid off at odds of 170 to 1. It led him and his sons to start again with a new family partnership, J. O. Hambro and Company – that bet, too, has paid off. A merchant banker needs to have courage and ought to have style. He had both. (25 June 1994)

Local boy makes good

It is 48 years since Dennis Weatherstone started work as a 16-year-old City clerk. Some prescient manager gave him a start at the Guaranty Trust of New York's London office. The Guaranty was merged into the Morgan bank and its rising star found his way to 23 Wall Street, where visiting Chancellors as far back as Denis Healey would come to learn about the markets from him.

Now Sir Dennis has retired as chairman of J.P. Morgan. He has seen its business transformed, from blue-chip lending to advanced financial engineering, but has striven to keep to what old Jack Morgan said it must do – first-class business done in a first-class way. The Bank of England has signed him up for its Board of Banking Supervision, but his connection might have been closer still. He is, so I learn, one of the very few people – Oliver Franks may have been the last – to have been sounded out for the Governorship and, politely, turned it down. (7 January 1995)

The age of gold

Joseph Kagan was best known as the manufacturer of the Gannex raincoat, often worn by his friend Harold Wilson.

A spiv writes: With the passing of Joe Kagan (Sir Joseph until he was crossed off the list, but indelibly Lord Kagan of Elland) we mourn the last survivor of those ampler days when politics and money met on easy terms. With the Prime Minister (now Lord Wilson of Rievaulx) he shared an interest in east–west trade, as did such fellow stalwarts as Lord Plurenden (now better known as Rudy Sternberg) and, of course, Bob Maxwell – Rudy hiding his light under a bushel, Bob as always a law unto himself! How I remember those happy evenings at the big house in Kensington Palace Gardens, with Joe crouching at the chessboard. How hurt he was when a short-lived Tory government expelled his favourite opponent on the specious grounds that he was a KGB agent.

Eric Miller was another kindred spirit – Sir Eric, as he became before his tragic end, precipitated by a disagreement with the auditors, so often a hazard in a public company. Joe never made that mistake and, although he was charged with theft, ultimately returning to face trial and imprisonment, he had done no more than to combine an ingenious scheme of tax avoidance with a justified impatience of exchange control and some creative invoicing. Lord Nolan's committee, now seeking to establish standards of probity in public life, should look back to the golden era of Joe Kagan. (28 January 1995)

A ghost writes

Nick Leeson is off to Singapore to complete the research on his book, 'Changi Cuisine: A Hundred Healthy Ways to Serve Fish-heads and Rice'. I shall not rush to read it, even though Edward Whitley will be writing it. Ed's cavalier style will be hard to adapt to Nick's estuarial English. The book I want to read will be Peter Baring's, and will be called: 'How We Let This Little Berk Bring the House Down'. It will explain how a risk-averse bank backed a man called Heath, who introduced it to new and thrilling business in the Far East and made it a whole lot of money. The bankers then sacked him and tried to run this business themselves, in the mistaken belief that (as they told the Bank of England) it was easy. Pleasantly surprising results, so Peter Baring called them, and pleasantly surprising bonuses all round, including a million for the chairman. Not a squeak from the owners, whose shares had no votes. Not a squeak from the Bank. Squeaks of warning from the markets, but the Barings thought they knew better. If I can reach suitable terms with Mr Baring I might write his book myself. (4 November 1995)

Impresario with a seamless mind

I went to lunch with Michael Von Clemm in the Mayfair town-house he had colonised for Merrill Lynch. French windows opened out onto a lawn and the catering was by the Roux brothers. It seemed – it was – a long way from Canary Wharf, the banking factory in deepest Docklands that had been his brainchild. This address, Michael thought, suited him better: 'So much more convenient for one's tailor, one's wine merchant, one's club, one's home and of course one's airport.' That was essential for the international financial markets' greatest impresario. He was constantly in flight. I once caught up with him in Washington, where he was feeding up some minute Mongolian central bankers. He had the entrée everywhere. When some treasurer made difficulties about seeing him, putting him off two or three times, Michael pulled a camera out of his pocket and took the man's picture: 'I wanted to be able to prove that you existed.'

He had been present at these markets' creation. Chance had brought him to that nursery of talent, the London office of the First National City Bank of New York, just as change was stirring around the City's bombsites and within its over-comfortable banking parlours. New markets in money and capital, knowing no frontiers but excluded from New York by clumsy regulation, were beginning the City's transformation to an offshore financial centre on Thames, and Michael's original and active mind was in its element. Michael thought seamlessly when so many of his contemporaries were keeping their ideas in watertight compartments. Up at Oxford, he had met the chief of the Washugga tribe, who was driving a Rolls-Royce and sounds like a Balliol man to me. This encounter prompted Michael, as an academic anthropologist, to spend two years in Washugga country on the slopes of Mount Kilimanjaro.

When he came to the City he was repelled by its cooking, which in those days featured custard. So he and his friends backed a pair of chefs who had cooked for the Rothschilds in London and Paris. He was the financial intellect behind the rise of Michel and Albert Roux to fame and stardom, as their restaurants won and kept an absolute majority of all the Michelin stars awarded in this country. Looking for a site for his bank's back office, he went to see a dusty dockside warehouse which had once held tomatoes, shipped from the Canaries. It occurred to him that he should leave the back office where it was and move the front office instead. By the time this happened he had, sensibly, changed banks.

From New York last year he called me to say that he had a hole in his head, after an operation for a tumour, brought on, so his doctors had told him, by long-distance flights and mobile telephones. He recovered and came back to academic life, as President of Templeton College, Oxford, but the tumour recurred and has killed him. There was and is no one like him. (15 November 1997)

A better class of enemy

The aptest tribute to Ian Hay Davison was the list of those not present when, this week, he collected the Founding Societies Award, his fellow accountants' highest accolade. These absentees were unavoidably detained, some by the Fraud Squad and some by the grim reaper. The crooks and fraudsters exposed by his efforts include John Stonehouse, the Labour minister turned banker turned round-the-world swimmer. Then came the autocrat of the Grays Building Society, and the chairman of the Hong Kong Stock Exchange, and the dark-suited bandits at Lloyd's of London. Put into Lloyd's to clean its rotten apples out, he soon discovered that something was wrong with the barrel. He fell out with the market's bluff, genial, untrustworthy chairman. Years and billions later, he was proved right about Lloyd's, and right about the chairman, whose career ended in disgrace. His award does him credit but his list of enemies is an award in itself. (16 May 1998)

City of refuge

I went to see Henry Grunfeld in the week of his ninetieth birthday and found him in his office, as always. His only concession to age was to stand down as president of SG Warburg, the bank that he and Siegmund Warburg founded. Relabelled as a senior adviser, he worked on for another five years until his death, a week ago. It used to get him into trouble, as he told me: 'We were rather blamed for starting work early. It wasn't to annoy people. It was just that we were used to that, on the Continent.'

He had been born into a dynasty of German steelmakers who lost their business when he and his father were summoned to Berlin and told by Ernst Roehm's Brownshirts to hand over. He was lucky to escape with his life: 'I was in hiding for weeks and weeks until I heard that the man who had arranged my arrest had been shot.' It was time to go, and he and Siegmund Warburg met in exile. Years later a young recruit asked him whether the two of them had planned what followed: 'I thought: you must have been to Harvard. I told him there was absolutely no planning. We had totally empty desks.' They had, too, in his words, the burning ambition and determination to show the world that they could do it. They did. To such men may the City of London always be a city of refuge. (19 June 1999)

No cheques, please

I am sure there has been some misunderstanding. Either the accounts of Hollis Industries are wrong or Geoffrey Robinson is wrong, so it must be the accounts. They say that he was paid £200,000 a year as chairman, but somebody might have written that in as a joke, rather like Auberon Waugh when he altered George Gale's name to Lunchtime O'Gale in the contents page of *The Spectator*. It is true that Mr Robinson signed the accounts, but he could not be expected to read every line, let alone the line about what he was paid. So there was nothing for him to declare, to the House of Commons, the Department of Trade's inspectors or anyone else.

Now that pesky fellow Tom Bower has turned up papers from Robert Maxwell's empire (Hollis was a province) which could be construed as an invoice for £200,000 and as an order to pay it. Perhaps this, too, was a spoof, or perhaps the cheque bounced and Mr Robinson wrote it all off to experience, which must have been helpful when he became Paymaster-General and signed the government's cheques. Or perhaps his denial is modelled on President Clinton's: I did not have cheques with that man. Read all about it in the *New Statesman* (publisher and proprietor, G. Robinson). (24 March 2001)

Easy does it

I hope that Stelios Haji-Ioannou has not started to inhale his own publicity. This is always a bad sign. EasyJet, the cut-price airline which charges for drinks but is quick on the draw with the trolley, has made him famous, and I began to worry when he picked a fight with Barclays Bank (of all opponents) over landing rights at Luton. Then came easyeverything, his chain of Internet cafés, and here comes easymoney. In partnership with London Scottish, a finance house which, like its customers, is not in the first rank, he is going into the credit card business, in which Barclays is the market leader. Meanwhile his airline's most advertised customers, the Blairs – those weathervanes – have switched to Ryanair. Easycome, easygo. (15 September 2001)

Jack the Lad

I lead a sheltered professional life. In the course of my work I have often adjourned from the boardroom to the luncheon-room, but never from there to the bedroom. I differ in this from the editor of the *Harvard Business Review*, who, when she went to interview 'Neutron Jack' Welch of General Electric, got on with him like a disorderly house on fire. Then the story came out, and Neutron Jack has sustained a nuclear counter-strike from Mrs Welch, who is suing for hundreds of millions of dollars, and the editor has temporarily stepped down.

'Dear Mr Fildes,' so the *Harvard Business Review* writes to me. 'Your career isn't just about money, is it? It's about something deeper. Something so central to what makes you tick that you can't imagine living without it.' At this point I made an excuse and left. (16 March 2002)

According to plan

It was towards the end of the last century that I nominated the Queen Mother as tax planner of the year. There was a silly fuss at the time about the overdraft she was supposed to have run up at Coutts. This, I said, would not worry her bank or its new chairman, Lord Home, in the slightest: 'It is sensible for a 98-year-old to finance herself by borrowing, rather than by selling assets, being caught for capital gains tax, selling more assets to pay the tax, and so on. Her overdraft can then be secured on these assets, and offset against them when estate duty finally has to be paid.' This strategy has now come to fruition, and the only loser is the tax office. In this way, as in so many, an example to us all. (6 April 2002)

There's more to good business than laws or codes or bankers' wheezes

Warren Buffett became chairman of Salomon Brothers by accident. The big swinging bankers there (evoked by Michael Lewis in *Liar's Poker*) had tried to swing a fast one on the United States Treasury and were caught, and were out – and since Berkshire Hathaway, Mr Buffett's company, was a major investor, he was left holding the baby. To the survivors he set out the old-fashioned standards he would now expect: 'Contemplating any business act, an employee should ask himself whether he would be willing to see it immediately described by an informed and critical reporter on the front page of his local paper, there to be read by his spouse, children and friends. We simply want no part of any activities that pass legal tests but that we, as citizens, would find offensive.'

Then time moved on and so did Mr Buffett, and a new generation of swinging bankers came to Wall Street and thought that his ideas about investment looked old-fashioned, too. Berkshire Hathaway searched for value and, when it found this, hung on to it, but stocks from the new world of dot.coms and telecoms offered something far better than value – they offered momentum. Besides, how could you measure value in a dot.com company which paid no dividends and had no earnings, no profits, no assets and as yet no sales? Well, you could find terms that flattered it. Bad terminology, so Mr Buffett warns us, is the enemy of good thinking: 'In golf, my score is frequently below par on a pro forma basis.' (11 May 2002)

Memo from Arnold

A memo came round from the managing director: 'All standing committees are by this direction disbanded. If you wish to confer with colleagues, by all means do so, but remember that you will be held personally responsible for any decision affecting your operating unit. Also remember that you are not obliged to join any such gathering. Incidentally, on this matter of personal responsibility, prior permission from HQ is required for any proposal to employ management consultants.'

This was the young Arnold Weinstock at GEC, and this was his style. Cash was controlled, performance was monitored, there were no hiding places. When he died this week, he had suffered the mortification of seeing his successors wreck his work – but how I wish he could come back to blast away all the clutter of committees and codes and consultants that now overrun British companies, sometimes in the sacred name of corporate governance, and to tell managers that they must get on and manage. There are 184 meeting rooms at British Airways' head office. At Arnold's HQ, so far as I know, there were none. (27 July 2002)

File and forget

Siegmund Warburg (1902–82) was the dominant City banker of his day and perhaps of his century. David Kynaston, historian of the City, ranks him with Nathan Meyer Rothschild – but on Monday, the new owners of the bank he founded will drop his name down the *oubliette*. UBS Warburg (the initials used to stand for Union Bank of Switzerland but no longer stand for anything) will become UBS Investment Bank. A sanctimonious letter to clients explains that putting them first 'will be the cornerstone of our re-branding', so Sir Siegmund will be laid to rest underneath it, unless, of course, he is revolving. (7 June 2003)

Tell us more

A note reaches me from the human relations empire: 'We are requesting information on ethnic origin and religious beliefs. This will enable us to comply with recent new discrimination legislation.' So will I kindly record my own ethnic origin, choosing from a list of 16 – Chinese perhaps, which subdivides into Chinese and Other? And my religion – Buddhist, Christian, Hindu, Sikh, None? What business all this is of anyone else, or how it contributes to making the company prosper, must be an open question, but it supports two bureaucracies, corporate and governmental, and helps them to make work for one another. That independent-minded banker Walter Salomon, of German-Jewish birth and a fierce fighter for his causes, when confronted with an official form requiring him to state his race, wrote 'Human'. (29 May 2004)

"Some boardrooms have potted plants in them and some have non-executive directors. The question in either case is: are they there for use or for ornament?"

CHAPTER FOUR

THE LEANING TOWER OF LIME STREET

The scandals and travails of Lloyd's of London

Lloyd's showy new building – high-tech on the outside, pencils and paper within – turned out to be the stage for high drama and dark deeds. An inflexible belief that its own ways were the best ways brought it to the verge of collapse. Like the BBC and the National Health Service, this was supposed to be a national institution so much admired that no other country had the nerve to copy it. Ten years ago I was arguing that Lloyd's best assets were or should be its name and its franchise, and that it ought to do more to trade on them and protect them. I was pleased, in the end, when Lord Levene, Lloyd's first chairman from outside the market, took the hint.

"_You can go to sea in a sieve, like the Jumblies, or you can join the wrong syndicate at Lloyd's of London._ **"**

Long view at Lloyd's

In 1981, the most successful syndicate was able to write its members a £4836 cheque for every £10,000 stake in its operations. The least successful – an aviation syndicate which seems to have skidded off the runway – had to ask each £10,000 stakeholder to send in a cheque for £17,029. 1985 ought to be a good year. We shall know in 1988. (27 April 1985)

All the wrong people

From 1988 onwards, the extent of Lloyd's troubles became evident.

Why, Sir Noel Coward would ask, do the wrong people travel? A similar lofty attitude can now be discerned in the high hall of Lloyd's: why do the wrong names join? More and more of them scramble to get in, crowding what once was an idiosyncratic private resort, insufficiently overawed by its splendours, changing its character, making a scene when the bill arrives – and even defying all tradition by refusing to pay it. Lloyd's now has more than 33,000 members, and there is talk of stiffening the qualifications for membership, requiring candidates both to show more means and to put down more cash.

It is a novel predicament for Lloyd's, which has spent most of the last 20 years putting word around that, exclusive club as it is, it might have room for a few more suitable members. In fact it was trying to repair its capital after the losses of the 1960s, when Hurricane Betsy cost the present-day equivalent of $7.5 billion. Lord Cromer, former Governor of the Bank of England, was asked to advise on capacity (the business Lloyd's could do governed by the money available to back it). Women were let in, and foreigners, and 'mini-names', with pocket-sized liabilities.

Today the average member of Lloyd's is a good deal more of a mini-name than his predecessor a generation ago, and more likely to be dependent on his reinsurance through 'stop-loss' policies, some of which are now the subject of serious dispute in the market. Today, suddenly, there is not enough good business to go round the membership, which has already learned to seek relief from the cost of unlimited personal liability, demanding to be bailed out by the Council or through the courts. Lloyd's ought now to consider how to raise the quality of the existing membership and shake the weaker names out. A special levy, to be paid by new members on joining – and distributed among those who resign? A market in membership, like the market in seats on exchanges? The positive response would be an active policy of opening up new business for Lloyd's to match the capacity, and that is now needed most of all. (16 January 1988)

Catharsis

Oh for a Lytton Strachey to chronicle Lloyd's of London! After *Eminent Victorians*, Noteworthy Citizens? He found a phrase to describe Oxford's parting with John Henry Newman which perfectly evokes Lloyd's parting with Ian Hay Davison, its chief executive , and another figure of inconvenient independence: 'The University breathed such a sigh of relief as usually follows the explosion of a hard piece of matter from a living organism.' Lloyd's could give us more encouraging, but scarcely more characteristic, signs of life. (30 November 1985)

Lloyd's freeloaders

Self-denying ordinance: I shall now try to stop teasing Lloyd's of London about their whizzing new building until they can persuade the Queen to come and see it. She was to have opened it, and one or two people rather hoped she might bring a sword with her, but she seems to be waiting until Sir Patrick Neill's investigation gives the all-clear, and that, if it comes, will not come much before Christmas. I do hope that all that Veuve Clicquot '79 in magnums does not maderise: Lloyd's, preparing for the royal occasion, cornered the market.

Another preparation has proved more economical. Lloyd's rightly decided that, in these uncertain times, it would no longer do to leave the floor open to anybody in a well-cut suit who would glance confidently at the waiter on the door, wish him a good morning, and stroll in. Lloyd's clamped down: admission by identity card. This, unexpectedly, showed that quite a lot of the chaps so busily dealing on the market's historic floor had never bothered to join, and were enjoying a free ride. Subscription incomes rose by three-quarters of a million pounds. At that rate, in a couple of hundred years they will have paid for the new building. (7 June 1986)

Wall game

From Lloyd's lost leader, Ian Hay Davison, comes a mine under the City's proliferating Chinese walls – the fortifications which will be supposed to stop a bank's investment managers getting together with its securities traders. Mr Davison, Lloyd's chief executive until his thunderous resignation, points out that the notorious PCW agency was bought by a broker under rules laid down by Lloyd's committee to prevent interference: 'The parent company was denied information about the subsidiary's activities, only one parent company director was allowed, and the agency's errors and omissions insurance was severed from that of its broker parent. Behind that perfect example of a Chinese wall, £40 million was abstracted from the Names.' Moral for City regulators and for bank directors: if you insist on the left hand not knowing what the right hand is doing, the right hand will creep into the till. (28 June 1986)

How Lloyd's could flourish in a cucumber frame, and stand its council on end

My advice to Murray Lawrence, the new chairman of Lloyd's of London, is: when all else fails, read the instructions. He should look again at the kit from which Lloyd's assembled Richard Rogers's prize-winning building. I think he will then find that it was put together the wrong way round or up. It ought to be lying on its side, like a cucumber frame. That would give Lloyd's what it obviously needs and has had for most of its history – a floor big enough to accommodate the market. Members would be saved that large part of their time which they now have to spend hopping from level to level on the escalators. ('Second floor, bullion, kidnap and ransom, space satellites, asbestosis, going down, please...') The council room would be left standing on end, but that would have advantages. (5 December 1987)

Tighten seatbelts

Times are getting harder at Lloyd's of London, where globe-flying brokers have found themselves demoted – from their accustomed first class, right down to business class. Over a glass of champagne in the Fenchurch Colony, an intrepid bird-man has been telling of the experience. 'Jolly exciting,' he says staunchly. 'Do you know, I could see the wings?' (12 March 1988)

When Lloyd's old-fashioned virtues have to be their own reward

Nobody likes paying out a billion dollars, and Piper Alpha is certainly the worst single loss in Lloyd's history. The response, all the same, shows Lloyd's old-fashioned virtues: it can pay, it does pay, it is prompt to pay. In off-the-peg standardised insurance Lloyd's will never compete with the mass producers. It must live by its skills at bespoke insurance, tailoring for risks with large, lumpy, individual, problem figures – like oil platforms. The loss underlines what Lloyd's chairman Murray Lawrence was telling his members at their annual meeting. They may have joined a tax-avoidance scheme, but now they are in an insurance market. (16 July 1988)

The Grobfather of Lloyd's

Lunch with the Grobfather was quite something. He made a grand entrance, supported by his butler, with a salver bearing a bottle of Dom Perignon and some cold silver pots. He then settled down to tell me how inadequately Lloyd's of London was managed – by a succession of underwriters who (he said) had never run anything bigger than their cosy family agencies. This was Kenneth Grob, the last of the big bad broker barons of Lloyd's, who has died in exile from the market which expelled him. He sold his barony to the Americans, and they noticed that he had left them £55 million short. In the end, the police noticed too. They brought him to trial seven years after the event, to spend months in court, facing a scatter-gun prosecution with a high proportion of misfires. The technique has become familiar, and its failure was deserved.

About Lloyd's, I have long thought he was right – in saying that it needed to be run like a business. If the penny has been slow to drop, that was partly Grob's fault. Lloyd's had first to concentrate on regulation, so as to stop its professionals spiriting the members' money away to Panama and the South of France. His lunchtime routine told its own story. I got a small warm dry sherry, The Dom Perignon was for him (an overrated champagne, I always think). (11 January 1992)

Cometh the hour and the man – here comes my bid for Lloyd's of London

The bid for the Midland Bank has given me the inspiration I need. I intend to bid for Lloyd's. Not Lloyds the bank, which is a success story and priced accordingly, but Lloyd's of London, the insurance market, whose members in their present mood might pay me to take it away. Some of them, indeed, would have to. That is only one of the novelties of my proposal, which will need skilful financial engineers and an ally with a deep pocket – perhaps the Swiss Re. The concept, though, is simple. Lloyd's, like the Midland, is a financial business with a fine old name and a valuable franchise, which went into a spiral of decline and has been trying to pull itself out – partly by its own efforts and partly on signs of improvements in its markets. That is the bidder's moment, as the Hongkong Bank (and Lloyds Bank too) saw when they looked at the Midland.

The bidder for Lloyd's of London has had much of his home-work done for him, free of charge, by his target. The report which the Council commissioned from David Rowland pinpoints Lloyd's weaknesses. Costs come first. Lloyd's, which used to run rings round the clumsy insurance companies, is now 30 per cent out of line on costs. Too many mouths are being fed too richly – indefensible in a business which is set to lose £1 billion. When I take over, there will be empty tables at the Marine Club. Rowland thinks that Lloyd's needs new capital from new sources, including companies. So it does, but it has not until now thought of my bid as a source. Rowland accepts that Lloyd's unique system of unlimited personal liability now does more harm than good, and has a complicated proposal which, in all but name, would end it. My proposal would end it more simply and at a stroke. (28 March 1992)

Those heady days on Lloyd's heavenly floor don't pass the Jefferson test

Thomas Jefferson, President of the United States, believed that any candidate who wanted the job should be disqualified from holding it. I would apply that rule to the chairmanship of Lloyd's of London. Its powers of seduction are too strong. An agreeable chap makes a play for the chair because he thinks (or his wife thinks) that it would be a good thing to have done, and a knighthood has been known to come with it. Then he is wafted up in the lift to the chairman's floor, which is like heaven, except that all revolves round him.

Below at a great distance through a glass wall, he can see the market's workaday world. Up here, all is calm. Massive furnishings soothe the nerves, mighty trophies bear witness to Lloyd's past. Deferential waiters in blue and red liveries map out the day: 'The Japanese delegation, chairman. Then the man who is painting your portrait. Then the programme for your visit to China. Then you are presenting a Lloyd's silver medal. This evening you are addressing the Mansion House dinner. Your speech is in your in-tray for your approval. White tie and decorations, chairman. Your car is at the door.'

Heady stuff. Chairmen can get carried away by it. They identify themselves with the grandeur of the institution, they are reluctant to believe that the wheels may be coming off, and no courtier in that monarchy will be specially eager to say so. (11 July 1992)

Franchising Lloyd's

What Lloyd's new management can and surely will do is to concentrate on Lloyd's best asset, which ought to be its name. If Lloyd's were a franchising operation, like The Body Shop, and instead of insurance sold banana conditioners, its name would have been better protected. A whole lot of duds, sharps, second cousins, free riders and nodding donkeys would have lost their right to it by now, leaving it to the professionals who would take care of it. Lloyd's has to set and enforce standards, not only of probity but also of competence, appropriate to the world's best-known name for insurance. Once it can do that, it could and should charge new investors a franchising fee for the use of the name. Lloyd's could always find a use for the money. (17 April 1993)

An elegant hole in the ground in EC3 – throw your money in here

I have a new and improved plan for Lloyd's of London. It fits in with my proposal to dismantle Lloyd's impractical head office, and re-erect it at Sydenham, on the site of the Crystal Palace. When it has gone, it will leave a large hole in the ground, conveniently located in the City. On the edge of this hole I shall put up a notice, which will say: THROW YOUR MONEY IN HERE. Below this, in smaller but still legible lettering, I shall add: AT YOUR OWN UNLIMITED RISK. It will go with a roar. People will come up from their country estates and take taxis from Paddington to Lime Street, EC3, with boxes full of money. Throwing it in will carry a marked social cachet. It will help the toilers at the bottom of the hole to pay for their expensive suits, and keep them in smoked salmon sandwiches. I shall recycle some of the money, which can be used to pay for school fees or holidays in the West Indies. These will serve as sprats to catch mackerel.

The great thing is to keep the money pouring in. This is technically known, I believe, as a Ponzi scheme, and can be made to work with pigs and even with British Government stock. Something of the kind seems to have worked very well, on the site of the hole, for a long time. Of course the time will come, as it has, when the second line of my notice turns out to mean what it says. Then there will be grief and umbrage and litigation. I shall excavate another hole, conveniently located near the Inns of Court. Beside it I shall put up another notice, which will say: NOW THROW YOUR MONEY IN HERE. (30 April 1994)

A hollow clang and a recorded excuse – Lloyd's gets resigned to it

The Lutine Bell, salvaged from HMS Lutine, which sank off the Dutch coast in 1799, was traditionally rung to announce the sinking of a ship insured at Lloyd's. It was to be rung an unprecedented three times by David Rowland in 1996 to symbolise the suffering of Names who had borne more than £8 billion of losses, and the successful launch of a new recovery plan for the market.

Lloyd's of London moved swiftly to restore confidence this week on news that the Lutine Bell has resigned. Underwriters returning to their wooden boxes in Lloyd's high-technology building noticed its absence shortly after lunch, and its loss was entered in the Accidents Book with a state-of-the-art quill pen. 'If only they knew where it was,' said a broker, 'they'd ring it.' The historic Bell had been a fixture at Lloyd's for a century, clanging once for bad news and (occasionally) twice for good news. Its resignation is the latest in a series of imperfectly explained departures from Lloyd's, whose chief executive got on his bike a week ago. He followed the head of regulation, the director of the Equitas project and the finance director who lasted a month – not to mention the deputy chairman who felt the need to spend more time with his lawyers.

By now Lloyd's has a drill for these things. Word was put out unattributably that there had been no rift with the Bell, that its work had been substantially completed, that it found Lloyd's demanding and difficult, that it had not really been up to the job, that it had gone native, that it had been made a good offer and that the new bell, promoted from Lloyd's twelfth-floor belfry, was a great improvement. Lloyd's has recorded this message and uses it on all occasions. Run to earth in Corney & Barrow's champagne bar, the Bell explained that it was overworked and thought it was time to move on. The place was a madhouse, it said. Members of some of Lloyd's better-known syndicates asked how they, too, could resign and move on, but the Bell's only response was a single hollow clang. (25 November 1995)

Unlimited liability

Sir Peter Green was a genial chairman of Lloyd's, even if his legacies include its show-off building and its misguided Act of Parliament. Now that he has died, he is unhappily remembered as the chairman who was later censured for discreditable conduct. As an underwriter, acting on his Names' behalf, he had developed a conflict of interest and omitted to protect them from it. He might have pleaded that they had been warned. Applicants to join Lloyd's are put through interviews and must satisfy the chairman that they know what they are doing. He had his own technique for this: 'Well, Mr Um, you understand that you'll be liable down to your last penny, for risks you've never heard of, something your underwriter's let you in for?' 'Oh, yes, Sir Peter.' 'Good, well, have you got a cheque book with you?' 'Er, yes, Sir Peter...' 'Then just sign a few blanks for me and pass it over – I'll keep it in my desk.' 'But, Sir Peter...' 'But you realise, don't you, that this is what Lloyd's is about?' That was telling them. (3 August 1996)

In Lloyd's secret garden of earthly delights, the odds are on the Nubian

To join Lloyd's of London, it has long seemed to me, is to be the traveller in the *Arabian Nights* who comes to a gateway where a monstrous Nubian stands on guard. Through the gateway the traveller can see a garden, where lovely girls are playing chess. It is explained to him that he can go into the garden and challenge one of the girls to a game. If he wins, there is no pleasure that she will deny him. If he loses, though, he must submit himself to the pleasures of the Nubian.

Travellers to Lloyd's who contemplate this bet need to know the odds. There ought still to be room for a few well-heeled punters who know what they are doing, but the traveller at the Old

Rectory will find out that Lloyd's is no place for him. The odds favour the Nubian. (29 March 1997)

The bell tolls

11 September 2001 saw the destruction of the World Trade Center in New York.

Lloyd's of London's glass and steel tower was evacuated on Tuesday as the news of disaster came in from America. Nobody bothered to ring the Lutine Bell on the way out, but the underwriters, as they milled around in Lime Street, must have wondered if it would be worth their while to go back in again. Their losses are all too obvious, but the disaster will bring other losses which are harder to measure. Businesses and people will be moved to keep their heads down. They will risk less, spend less, travel less and stay at home. The barriers will stop coming down and will start to go up again. There will be losers from that close to home, among the leaders of the international money and capital markets, in the City of London and its glass and steel appendage in Canary Wharf. They represent globalisation in action, and if it is under threat, so are they. (15 September 2001)

Squire insurance

How not to insure a tower block: assemble a few thousand squires from the shires and let them run the risks. They would trade, each for himself and not one for another, in a club which had a shelf-life of a year. This annual joint venture would then be wound up, the books would be closed two years later and the profits, if any, distributed. The squires, who would be called 'names', would supply their own capital, and accept unlimited personal liability if the tower block fell down. They would sell their pictures and hunters and write cheques for billions of dollars. Every year a new club would be formed and the process would start again.

This is how Lloyd's of London did business for more than three centuries, making it one of those quintessentially British institutions which are supposed to be so much admired that no one copies them. It no longer makes sense and Lloyd's ruling Council has finally said so. The trouble is that Lloyd's tends to reform itself only when it is sufficiently frightened. It has been losing market share for years, and money, too, but the collapse of the towers in New York has sent premiums soaring, and the surviving Names have been told by their trade union, the Association of Lloyd's Members, that happy days are here again. Some Lloyd's professionals still make a good living as the Names' agents, and have resisted reform before now, seeing off a prospective chairman who wanted to do away with the annual joint venture. By now, though, fewer than 2,500 Names are still underwriting, and all that remains is to put a price on their nuisance value. (26 January 2002)

Lloyd's-on-sand

This is where I came in. Ian Hay Davison arrives to sort things out and to set standards. This upsets the old guard, who like things the way they are and can't see what is wrong with them. The pressure builds up, an explosion follows, he leaves, the old guard relaxes...

It happened, two decades ago, at Lloyd's of London and now it has happened again in Dubai, which is trying to set itself up as a financial centre and had drafted him in as regulator-in-chief. He was concerned about possible conflicts of interest on the new centre's governing body, but seems to have been told that, in a small place like Dubai, with a gene pool to match, things were different. Oh yes? At Lloyd's he had thrown out enough rotten apples to make him wonder if there was something wrong with the barrel. Soon enough his fears were vindicated. Lloyd's ran into every sort of trouble and came close to ruin, and the job of cleaning and reconstructing the barrel had to be done all over again. I used to say that Lloyd's motto, officially *Fiducia* – trust – was really *E cosa nostra*: it's our business. If that turns out to be the Dubai gene pool's motto, it will do nothing to inspire trust in Lloyd's-on-Sand. (26 June 2004)

Long-term risk

'Poor old Lloyd's,' said the underwriter, gesturing at the contraption of pipes and tubes which is the market's new home. 'After 300 years... We started off in a coffee-house and finished up in a coffee-percolator.' (26 April 1986)

CHAPTER FIVE

GOVERNORS AND CHANCELLORS

From Montagu Norman and Winston Churchill to Mervyn King and Gordon Brown – and even Che Guevara

The Bank of England and the Treasury have always been the best of enemies. Always? Well, at intervals since 1694, when the Bank got its charter from King William III. (The Treasury likes to trace itself back to the Plantagenets.) I have enjoyed watching this tense double act played out between Governors and Chancellors, blame deftly shifted, authority ceded and retrieved. It was a powerful Chancellor, Nigel Lawson, who proposed independence for the Bank – 'as if Cromwell,' I said, 'having driven the Irish to Hell or Connaught, had offered them Dominion status.' Another, Gordon Brown, went on to grant it, but on his own terms. Not all Chancellors were of this calibre, and one Deputy Governor ended up on the carpet.

Winston v. Monty

Nigel Lawson (now Lord Lawson of Blaby), Chancellor of the Exchequer 1983–89;
Robin Leigh Pemberton (now Lord Kingsdown), Governor of the Bank of England
1983–93; Winston Churchill, Chancellor 1924–29; Montagu Norman, Governor
1920–44.

The Robin and Nigel Show was always bound to run and run. Sixty years ago, the theme was the same and only the cast was different – it was then the Winston and Monty Show. The spring of 1926 saw Montagu Norman, Governor of the Bank of England, raise the Bank rate first and tell the Chancellor, Winston Churchill, later. Churchill was furious. The Treasury (and this is where the script has changed) tried to calm him down. The Controller of Finance, Sir Otto Niemeyer, wrote to a colleague:

> Winston will never realise that he is not Governor of the Bank. As regards Parliament, W. is absolutely entitled to say that it has never been the practice of the Bank of England, an independent bank fixing its own discount rate, to consult the Treasury, that it did not do so on this occasion, and that there was no reason why it should have. He would be very foolish to dissociate himself from sound finance by denouncing the Bank. The effect on national credit abroad would be exceedingly bad, and many of the good effects of the high rate, e.g. retention of balances here and improvement of exchange, would be undone.

Niemeyer has a lesson for our own times: if we are going to put up interest rates to defend sterling, it will be more effective and, in the end, cheaper to do it as if we mean it. But there was no reconciling Churchill to a two-man act in which his was the straight or supporting role. His resentment of Norman and the Bank grumbled on. Unable to help the Polish leader, Sikorski, over a matter of blocked funds in wartime, he explained: '*Quand je suis en face de la Vieille Dame de Threadneedle Street, je me trouve tout a fait impotent.*' (13 April 1985)

The King is dead

Lord Cobbold, Governor 1949–61

They no longer make Governors of the Bank of England like Lord Cobbold, who died this week – because the office and the Bank have changed, but also because Cobbold, more than any other Governor, had been able to prepare himself for the part over many years, had formed a clear view of it and disciplined himself to fit it. He was Montagu Norman's protégé and in a sense his heir, Norman spotted him deftly clearing up a financial mess in Italy, and brought him into the Court of the Bank in his early thirties. He was at once *papabile*. For the Bank, he handled the discussions which led to its nationalisation, and made no secret in later years of his pleasure in having out-manoeuvred the Treasury.

The critics who wanted the Bank reined in – Nicholas Davenport, in whose column I humbly tread, high among them – found that the Bank's autonomy seemed more secure than ever, on its new base. Cobbold's style made that possible. He was a monarch, conscious of the dignity and authority of his office, taking the great decisions himself, fortified by his professionalism, appearing wholly indifferent to others' opinions of him, finding no necessity to explain himself – though he would never have said, as Norman said: 'I don't have reasons, I have instincts.' He preferred to say little in public, to have the City's potentates come to him, to keep his dealings with government behind closed and sound-proofed doors. It was late in his reign before the critics broke in on him, and brought the Bank into the open at the 'Bank rate tribunal' and the Radcliffe inquiry into the monetary system. From that day to this have followed a series of attempts to nationalise the Bank again and do it properly. Cobbold preferred to exchange the Court of the Bank of England for the Court of the House of Windsor.

He was a formidable ruler in his own court – and capable of surprises. A Bank official, then junior, was asked with his wife to a reception where Cobbold would be present. 'What,' she asked, 'does the Governor look like?' The official rashly replied, 'He's a funny little man with glasses.' When the imposing figure of

Cobbold loomed up, she was sufficiently startled to say that she had expected a funny little man with glasses. Cobbold crouched down and jammed his spectacles on the end of his nose. 'Look,' he said, 'I'm a funny little man with glasses.' (7 November 1987)

Harold v. Rowley

Lord Cromer, Governor 1961–66

Nicholas Davenport, my sainted predecessor in this column, recorded that he once found Harold Wilson as a new Prime Minister with his feet, in new suede shoes, on the Cabinet table. Between puffs at his pipe he was grumbling about 'Rowley' Cromer, Governor of the Bank of England: 'You know, Nicholas, I had to take control of the little affair with the Governor. We had a proper confrontation in this room. I heard what he had to say – you know the stuff about freezing wages and cutting government expenditures. So I said: "Mr Governor, I would like to ask you one question. Who is governing Britain? The Governor of the Bank or the Prime Minister?" [Puff! Puff!] He didn't like it. [Puff! Puff!] No banker likes being deflated. They like to impose deflation on others.' Both were committed defenders of sterling, Cromer *ex officio* and Wilson as a matter of political decision. Sterling, of course, lost. (22 April 1995)

All at sea with Nigel

Nigel Lawson, Chancellor 1983–89

I have been wrong all this time about Nigel Lawson's tie. Not, that is, his pink-and-green club tie for moments of ebullience, but the conservative effect in dark blue which signals caution. I thought and, the other day, wrote that it was the Royal Naval Volunteer Reserve tie. Not so – it is the far more exclusive tie of the Coastal Forces Veterans Association, whose 1600 members (so the treasurer, Charles Milner, courteously explains to me) served in the Royal and allied navies in motor gunboats, launches, torpedo boats or in their shore bases. Most have wartime service, but Mr Lawson qualifies from his time in the 1950s as a naval Sub-Lieutenant in command of H.M. motor torpedo boat *Gay Charger*.

Those who served with Sub-Lt Lawson speak of his navigational skills (even up the trickiest creek), which were good enough to get many of his friends through their examinations. (10 December 1988)

Rising damp

Nigel the captain and Robin the first mate are sitting in their boat, which is leaking. Robin's feet have got wet, but he cannot bale the boat out, because Nigel has confiscated the baler and is sitting on it. Robin opens the subject diplomatically. 'The seas are so big,' he says, 'and our boat is so small. Do you think our boat is sinking?'

'On the contrary,' says Nigel, 'it's floating. That's what it's meant to be doing. Sometimes it floats up and sometimes it floats down. So long as we keep it properly trimmed, we don't have to bale it or steer it. That's all in the strategy.'

The water is up to Robin's shins. 'I've heard a forecast,' he says hopefully, 'that we shall soon be 10 per cent nearer the Plimsoll line.'

'I've heard it too, and it must be right sometime,' says Nigel, emptying barrels of crude oil over the stern. 'It's not our fault if there's too much oil on troubled waters.'

Robin mutters that for the price of that oil they could have bought another baler. 'Can't we head up into the swell?' he says. 'When I was a midshipman, the first mates would be steering 12 per cent or 15 per cent to starboard by now.'

'So they would,' says Nigel, 'but we know better. We're on the right course, so why should we change it? Anyway, if we're lower in the water, our cargoes will get to foreign ports quicker, because there will be less resistance.'

'I thought that if we got the trim right, the boat would look after itself...'

'Belay there, Mr Mate.'

Robin's discomfort is creeping up. 'How would it be,' he asks, 'if we got the life raft inflated? I mean, there seems to be quite a lot of...'

'What did I tell you about the trim?' snaps Nigel.

His mate splashes to attention and salutes, looking like a U-boat commander making a final gesture of chivalry. It would be a good part for Gregory Peck, just as the captain's would be a good part for Charles Laughton in his *Bounty* period. 'Sir,' says Robin, 'previous first mates, and previous captains, have found that by the time they were up to their necks in the water, they had to do something about it, whether they liked it or not.'

'I hear you, Mr Mate,' says Captain Nigel, 'and I'm sorry about the leak at your end of the boat.'

'Aye, aye, Sir,' says the mate. (5 January 1985)

Nigel's parting shot

Nigel Lawson's resignation caught me with steam up on the Watercress Line. It was and is a day to remember. I had been happily chuffing along some preserved railways on the *Daily Telegraph*'s business, and on getting home was surprised to be rung up by Max Hastings, the editor. 'Lawson's resigned,' he said. Shaken to the buffers, I asked what he wanted me to do. 'Put down that telephone,' came the word of command, 'and start writing.'

In the year that has followed, Nigel Lawson has, contrary to his nature, remained almost silent. Even his old enemy Sir Alan Walters was left to make a fool of himself without assistance. Now he has marked the anniversary in his old style, which runs to surprises and, preferably, ambushes. He turned up in the Commons to ambush the Prime Minister, without needing to name her – how pleased he was that she had taken his advice about the European Monetary System, what a pity she hadn't taken it when he first gave it, how much trouble she'd have saved... A parting shot from ambush, for he has told his constituents that he will not stand again.

So ends the extraordinary political career which I saw at its beginning, 20 years ago, when he was motoring past the playing-fields of Eton in a loudspeaker van, broadcasting his patchy campaign song: 'Eton and Slough, Eton and Slough! We want Nigel, we want him now...' Eton and Slough didn't though, but, by the 1974 election, he was the candidate for a safe seat, had written much of his party's manifesto and, I think, had been promised that he would go straight into office. On election night, learning that he was in Parliament but that his party was out, he rushed across the polished hall of his new house (now for sale) at Stony Stanton, and had the misfortune to tread where his secretary's spaniel, Lupin, had left a turd. He suffered a crash landing. The secretary, with marked presence of mind, cried: 'Oh, don't you realise, Mr Lawson, that's a sign of good luck!' He was not persuaded. (27 October 1990)

Someone to blame – at last a credible role for the incredible Chancellor

Norman Lamont (now Lord Lamont of Lerwick), Chancellor 1991–93

Norman Lamont on his way to 11 Downing Street looked a happy man. Lunching at the Savoy on that November day in 1990, I bumped into him as he bustled down the long corridor, grinning all over his face – and there, I thought, goes a man who has been given the job he always wanted. What a Greek gift it was. The recession had arrived, credit was drying up, sterling was shaky, and we had just joined the European Exchange Rate Mechanism – the coup that was to restore confidence in British policy and make the next election winnable. It backfired.

We had put our monetary policy out to contract to the Bundesbank, through the ERM, and were stuck with the consequences. Mr Lamont tried to get through on his face. At every opportunity, in fierce declamation and in careful argument, he proclaimed his utter commitment to the ERM and to the exchange rate at which we had joined. 'The Chancellor,' so I wrote in July, 'has staked his job on it. He should be worried to see the market take his bet and raise the stakes.' I took him to have made the ERM commitment a resigning matter. We soon found out. 'Black Wednesday' saw his policy destroyed in the markets – a total defeat, no less costly and humiliating if the policy was, as I thought, wrong. I assumed that the Chancellor would go with it.

I, though, was off to Washington for the International Monetary Fund meeting, where I found to my astonishment that Mr Lamont would be joining us. There he was, his usual chippy and chirpy self, perched in the rose garden of Dumbarton Oaks, singing (so he told us) in his bath, blandly explaining that he would now set his policy by what was happening in the British economy. 'What Mr Lamont's new policy needs,' I wrote, 'is a credible Chancellor.'

That remained his trouble, and the Government's and the economy's troubles, to the end. He cut interest rates. He got past the Conservative conference by wrapping himself in the Union Jack. He announced a strategy for growth (what a novel idea) and a target for inflation. What we needed, I thought, was a policy to make devaluation work, but that would mean austerity – Stafford Cripps' watchword and his style, but not really Norman Lamont's.

He went gaily on to unveil public spending plans which would mean borrowing £44 billion. He had tackled the easy option, cutting interest rates, but left the hard one, cutting spending, for another day and, as it proved, another Chancellor. Time was already running out for him. Last month I found myself drafting a job specification for a sit. which would soon become vac. – a financial director to take responsibility for a budget of £290 billion: 'The need now is for a strong external candidate, who will not be the captive of his staff and will make changes of his own. Nor will an inoffensively safe pair of hands suffice for the hard and unpopular choices that will have to be enforced. This is a job for a bruiser.'

Now we have one. What he has to do is evident. Mr Lamont, even if he had the will, no longer had the clout to do it. Kenneth Clarke is a luckier man. Best of all, he will have what Mr Lamont never had – a predecessor he can blame. That is the outgoing Chancellor's last service, and the curtain line in a small personal tragedy. (5 June 1993)

Man of Kent

Robin Leigh-Pemberton, Governor 1983–93

Now Robin Leigh-Pemberton will be spending more time with his railway. It runs (steam-hauled, of course) through his grounds at Torry Hill in Kent, and will now get the care and maintenance it needs. Near it is the tree stump where an estate worker once came across a mobile telephone, furiously quacking: 'It's Nigel Lawson speaking – put me through to the Governor.' 'I don't know about that, sir, I just found this thing 'ere.'

Governors need to be blessed with a sense of proportion. This one came in on a sticky wicket. Margaret Thatcher was suspicious of the Bank, on stiff terms with its Governor and no terms with its Deputy, who thought that her Medium Term Financial Strategy was a snake-oil remedy and said so. She seized the chance to make an appointment of her own – someone who, she thought, would be there to stand up for the right even if the election went wrong. That piece of casting was no help to Robin Leigh-Pemberton. He was caricatured as an unqualified political placeman, Downing Street's man in Threadneedle Street. He refuted that in action.

His legacy as Governor has been to move the Bank towards independence. Former Chancellors now fall over each other to say that the nation's credit would stand far more highly if he and not they were in charge. That is the best and least-sought compliment to a Governor who will now be happy to spend more time on his other job, as Lord Lieutenant of Kent. (26 June 1993)

Rupert on the carpet

Rupert Pennant-Rea resigned as Deputy Governor after his mistress, Mary Ellen Synon, told the press that they had made love on the carpet of the Governor's dressing room.

I opposed Rupert Pennant-Rea's appointment to the Bank of England in this column two years ago, I said that this was a job for a banker and a manager, and that he was not evidently qualified as either. He might, I said, be a splendid fellow, a fountain of ideas and a breath of fresh air (everybody said so), but this would no more qualify him to be Deputy Governor than to fly a Boeing 747. He had been plucked from the *Economist*, which, I thought, had been wrong on the major issues of policy with which the Bank had been concerned – but that was another story. It was the appointment, not the man, that worried me. Formally, it was

made by the Queen on the advice of the Prime Minister. In practice, it was a disgracefully scamped piece of work at 10 and 11
Downing Street.

In the event Mr Pennant-Rea settled down to the unfamiliar job
of a chief operating officer, under a dominant Governor. He was
little seen outside the Bank's windowless walls. He carried through
its reorganisation, which, though painful, was at least swifter and
defter than the Treasury's. He might have been remembered for it,
until now. Now he has been brought down, not on any issue of
public policy or competence, but by private folly (he says) and
personal vengeance. The result is a humiliation, for Mr Pennant-
Rea and for the Bank of England, and I regret it for them both.

To avoid any repetition of this incident, I understand that the
Board of Banking Supervision is conducting an inquiry and will be
publishing a code. It is already clear, as the Bank's supervisory
director Brian Quinn says, that there was a severe and rather dra-
matic breakdown of control. Headings from the new code will, so
I learn, include: (i) Not in the office. (ii) Well, not in the boss's
office, or his dressing room either. (iii) At least 18 inches above
floor level. (iv) What's wrong with the good old blotter? (v) Not
with financial journalists. (vi) Certainly not with obscure freelance
financial journalists who need to make a bob or two. (vii) Former
financial journalists should not need to be told this. (viii) The
standard principles of banking prudence – large exposures, four-
eyes monitoring – will apply to those transactions. (ix) Self-regulation makes you go blind. (25 March 1995)

What Gordon Brown needs is a soothing holiday beside a Dulwich birdbath

Gordon Brown, Chancellor 1993– ; Eddie George, Governor 1993–2003

The Treasury wonders whether the word 'holiday' is in
Gordon Brown's vocabulary. There is talk of a dash to Cape
Cod, but he would have to hurry back to go abroad again. In
September he has meetings that will take him as far as Hong Kong.
He is caught up in a hectic round of news making, some genuine,
some factitious. He had trouble this month finding time for his

Budget, and it was a rushed job, as became apparent. Now he should give himself and his staff and the rest of us a break, and if he wants a destination I can recommend the leafy charms of Dulwich.

Eddie George is holidaying there this week – he lives there – and the two of them could have soothing chats around the Georges' birdbath. Relations between Chancellor and Governor are tense. Their honeymoon began when Mr Brown gave the Bank of England powers to set interest rates, and ended when he took away its powers to do much of what it does now. The details are being argued out amid muttered complaints about breaches of trust. Mr Brown's news managers have been no help. Conspiracy theorists say that Mr George has been stuck with the unpopular but necessary task of raising interest rates, and when he has done that he can go. As Kipling so nearly put it: 'Oh, it's Eddie this, and Eddie that, and Eddie, go away, But it's "Thank you, Mr Governor" when the band begins to play.' Mr Brown should add this to his holiday reading, together with the *Michelin Guide to South East London*. (26 July 1997)

George 1, Dragon 0

Governors of central banks are a threatened species. There are only 172 of them in the world, but last year 29 of them lost or quit their jobs. In the previous year 35 of them left, only three of them at the end of their terms. These alarming figures (from the *Morgan Stanley Central Bank Directory*, which is the spotter's handbook) underline Eddie George's feat of survival in getting himself nominated for another term when his runs out in June. He had some tense moments last summer, but later on his colleagues noticed that his hair was curling and assumed that all was well. His constituency is the financial markets, which will cheer his return, as ministers have had the sense to realise. (21 February 1998)

Hush in the Close

One of the pleasures of my work was to watch Nigel Lawson at the wicket, facing the bowling of the House of Commons Treasury Committee. Brian Sedgemore hurled bouncers at him and he stood up to them. A white-headed Liberal called Wainwright somehow provoked him to hit his harmless half-volleys out of the ground. Anthony Beaumont-Dark would charge in, full of fire: 'Let me tell you, Chancellor, that in the Midlands, where we still make things...' 'Oh, are you a manufacturer, Mr Beaumont-Dark? I always thought you were a stockbroker.' Then Nick Budgen would come on from the Victoria Tower end. Line, length and spin; a deceptive action; pinpoint accuracy; the batsman intensely focused, watching each delivery on to the bat; a breathless hush in the Close.

It says something about politics that in all the long years of Conservative government, Nick Budgen was never picked for the Treasury team, although as time went on it certainly attracted its fair share of duds and duffers. He was inconveniently right about its policies, about inflation and about our venture into the exchange rate mechanism – and on Europe and its single currency, he has been looking righter by the week. Now he is dead. I would like to believe that in today's House of Commons, there is someone as skilled and as awkward as he was in searching Chancellors out. (31 October 1998)

Message from Mauritius

A message in a bottle drifts in from Mauritius, where my man in the beach bar saw Gordon Brown take to the air: 'It's a bird, it's a plane, it's Superchancellor!' The Treasury has now confirmed that he flipped round the island in a helicopter and then chartered not one but two aircraft to go on to his next meeting. He had joined the Commonwealth finance ministers in Mauritius 15 months ago, coming hotfoot from a meeting of Europe's finance ministers in Luxembourg, and his incoming flight (British Airways) was held up. If he had been driven from the airport to the meeting, my man tells me, he would have been late for the opening ceremony and missed his chance to appear in the group photograph. A helicopter was the answer, and he took to it, twice at the Mauritian police's expense and twice at the British tax-payers'.

When it came to getting off the island, my man says, the other four dozen ministers and their bag carriers did it the easy way. They hopped onto the plane that Air Mauritius had provided to fly them straight on to the International Monetary Fund meeting in Hong Kong. This, though, was not good enough for Gordon Brown. He wanted to travel by way of Bangkok, where he had booked himself in to address the Asia Europe meeting, such as it was. So he chartered a plane to pick up a connection in Johannesburg, but had to put down in Madagascar to refuel, and missed his connection, and flew to Singapore instead and char-tered another plane, all in the cause of duty. I shall find it my duty to check up on him at this year's meeting of Commonwealth finance ministers, which will be conveniently located in the Cayman Islands. (13 February 1999)

Monty's double

Leslie O'Brien (later Lord O' Brien of Lothbury), Governor 1966–73

I try to imagine Montagu Norman appearing on *Breakfast with Frost*: 'Would it be fair to say, Governor, that the dogs barked and the caravan moved on?' 'Yes, David, but I don't have reasons, I have instincts.' Nowadays this is part of the job at the Bank of England, and Sir Edward George does it manfully. No doubt he takes his line from another Governor, Leslie O'Brien, long schooled in crisis management. 'A major duty of every central banker,' O'Brien recalled, 'is to learn how to exude confidence without actually lying.' (29 September 2001)

The Gordon and Prudence Show is nearing the end of its run

One more Budget and Gordon Brown will go on to chal-lenge Gladstone. He is coming up for his seventh year as Chancellor and by now we know the Gordon and Prudence Show so well that we can hum along with him. That delivery, as insistent as a road drill, the plonking catchphrases, the tortured arithmetic, the fidgety initiatives, the sinking realisation that we shall have to labour for longer to meet his demands – this is his formula, and he has come to rely on it.

Only a year ago it got him hailed as the wonder-working Chancellor who could meet all society's needs. Back on stage for his encore this week, he must have sensed a change of mood. The show has begun to degenerate into self-parody. It now includes a Trades Union Learning Fund and an enhanced fuel allowance for the over-80s. A rustling of plush can be heard under corporate behinds in the stalls. Further back, those who have to buy their own tickets are finding it harder, and from the seats supposedly packed with supporters comes the impatient sound of whistling. Some people, he must reflect, are never satisfied. What is the matter with them? Is it just that they have got bored with his formula and want another script, or have they found fault with the strategy that has taken him and his party so far for so long? This week he looks fallible. (12 April 2003)

Mervyn's in goal and Gordon's moved the posts
Mervyn King, Governor 2003–

Poised on the Bank of England's line, Mervyn King, its Governor, stands ready to save us from the penalty goal of inflation. He has been heard to grumble that Gordon Brown has moved the goalposts. Inflation is now to be measured by a new index, of the Chancellor's choice, which leaves the bad news (housing costs, council tax) out to great effect. His new inflation rate, at 1.3 per cent, is only half the old one. Never mind, says Mr King, the Bank thinks it will work its way upwards and come out in two years' time at 2 per cent, where it would hit the Chancellor's new target. Just to keep it on track, Mr King and his colleagues raised Bank rate last week, to applause from the Treasury end. Ed Balls waved his scarf in support and Gordon Brown urged the Bank on to do it again: 'We will continue to support our monetary authorities in the difficult choices they have to make.'

First he moves the goalposts, then he second-guesses the goal-keeper – this is the Chancellor who memorably gave the Bank its independence, but second-guessing is second nature to him and he can leave nothing alone for too long. One of these days the Bank and the Treasury will fall out – they always do – and the Governor will find himself at cross purposes with the government. That will be the test of Mr King's mettle, and of the Bank's independence. (14 February 2004)

Sorry, Gordon

We must commiserate with Gordon Brown, who this week overhauls David Lloyd George to become the longest-serving Chancellor since Gladstone. He is so obviously anxious to move over before his effects come unstuck – as happens to Chancellors who stay too long – and to follow his mighty predecessors into the house next door. The Treasury said of Lloyd George that he used figures as though they were adjectives. This Chancellor likes to use them as though they were baseball bats, but the ones to spot are the ones he leaves out. The Blessed Prudence, virgin and martyr, helped with these deceptions until he gave her the cold shoulder. No Chancellor has spent so much of our money, and few, perhaps, to less effect, but if he stays on he may yet learn from Gladstone. Wealth, so the greatest of chancellors said, should be allowed to fructify in the pockets of the people. (19 June 2004)

Governor Che

Keep faith with the revolution – idolise a central banker! I am inspired to learn that Che Guevara, pin-up of successive student radicals and activists, was briefly Governor of the Central Bank of Cuba. Banknotes with his signature command a premium, which puts them as close as the Cuban peso gets to a sound currency. It is a pity that his country never joined the International Monetary Fund, or we might have met on the annual circuit in Washington, popping out for a Cuba Libre and discussing regulatory policy. One way and another a missed opportunity. Now what I want is a pin-up poster of Montagu Norman. (19 August 2000)

Comrade Governor

My revelatory discovery that Che Guevara was Governor of the Central Bank of Cuba has been confirmed. 'I have long enjoyed the fact that Che was a fellow-member of the banking fraternity,' writes Sir Kit McMahon, who was Deputy Governor of the Bank of England. 'Seated round the camp fire in the mountains, with Havana about to capitulate before them, Castro and his colleagues were sorting out portfolios. At the end the Leader remembered that they hadn't filled the post of governor of the central bank, and asked the group: "Is anyone here an economist?" Che thought he said "Communist", put up his hand and got the job.' In the fraternity, Sir Kit and I have seen worse appointments. (2 September 2000)

CHAPTER SIX

THE BOONDOGGLE CIRCUIT

The curious world of multinational talking shops and conferences

What do Governors and Chancellors do? They go to meetings. They must have air miles coming out of their briefcases. These meetings, and the international bureaucracies that keep them going, and the parties that go with them, came to obsess me. Where are they held? Well, more probably Cancun than Wolverhampton. What should be be on the agenda? When and where to meet next. World economic summits, which became the most elaborate charades of all, began over rounds of whisky in the White House library. I would watch with fascination as a meeting spawned a secretariat and hatched out as an international agency, with a marble hall to house it. The whole process was so much easier to start than to stop. Should the World Bank be told to work itself out of a job? Perhaps, but if there were no meetings, what would happen to the parties?

Boondoggle: coined 1929 by Robert H. Link (d. 1957) American scoutmaster. (1) A braided cord worn by Boy Scouts as a neckerchief slide, hatband, or ornament. (2) A wasteful or impractical project or activity, often involving graft. (Merriam-Webster's Dictionary)

London gets the Berd, but will it be a thinnifer or a fattipuff?

An eminent central banker once explained to me the difference between the International Monetary Fund and the World Bank. 'The thing is, Christopher,' he said, 'the Fund are thinnifers and the Bank are fattipuffs.' Hapless Bank, put on a strict diet only the other day, already expanding again on an afflatus of feminism, busily commissioning studies on the role of women in the process of structural adjustment, and yet positively slender and athletic beside such sluggards as Unctad – Under No Circumstances Take Any Decisions!

Now to the ranks of these international agencies comes the Berd, the European Bank (getting its acronym from Banque Européenne) for Reconstruction and Development. A thinnifer Berd or a fattipuff? That will be the test. The pace and commitment which have brought the Berd so far suggest a thinnifer. Six months from the breach in the Berlin Wall, and 40 countries have committed themselves to put up the Berd's capital and have agreed on the Berd constitution, on a pecking order of shareholders – the IMF can spend years and years on that – and even on who should head it (President Mitterrand's guru, Jacques Attali) and where it should be (London). If that pace can be sustained, another 12 months should see the Berd up and laying.

No one doubts that there is urgent work to be done. What matters is whether the Berd can do it. Other agencies, notably the International Finance Corporation (a World Bank offshoot), are already at work in Eastern Europe. Will weak economies be able to play off one agency against another, as Argentina played off the World Bank against the IMF? Will the new bank have more to contribute than the existing Development Banks for Asia and Africa – which would not be saying much?

As for the philosophic M. Attali – that wholly unofficial biographer of Siegmund Warburg and author of a history of time, incorporating notions which had previously occurred to Jung, Marx and Voltaire, and notable, as a reviewer complained, for a tragic absence of quotation marks – his presence guarantees that the Berd will be distinctive, but not that it will fly. (26 May 1990)

Knock, knock! Who's there? Attali. Attali who? Attali and completely over the top

The Berd has certainly come a long way in the 14 months since it was first a gleam in François Mitterrand's eye. The Berlin Wall had been breached, peaceable revolutions were spreading eastwards across Europe, the West held its breath and then launched a fund. That is a familiar reflex response to momentous events; the quarrels tend to come later, as they have. By the spring, the Berd had £7 billion promised, from the 40 countries which are shareholders. It had a home – so that London, at long last, housed a big international agency – and a president. No one could say that Jacques Attali was just another financial bureaucrat. He was M. Mitterrand's guru, a man of ideas.

His ideas for the Berd were on a grand scale. His search for a suitably grand head office started off with Grand Buildings, in Trafalgar Square. There he tried and failed to gazump Enterprise Oil. He resisted the Treasury's attempts to shoo him down to the Isle of Dogs where eastern Europe begins. He agreed to take over the Midland Bank's head office, a Lutyens palace, but could not have it altered to suit him. M. Attali's next symptom of corporate ambition was to call for a logo. He invited the world's schoolchildren to compete in designing one for him. Vaclav Havel and Issey Miyake, with help from Sir Nicholas Goodison, would pick the winner. (It looks like a tennis ball.) A head of merchant banking is still being sought, but M. Attali's personal chef (French, of course) is already in place. (20 April 1991)

Cher Jacques…

The annual meeting of the European Boondoggle for Remuneration and Disbursement, in London early next week, will inaugurate a régime of austerity. Arriving on his personal bicycle, Jacques Attali, the president, will offer delegates *les sandwiches Marmite du chef* washed down by *le thé à l'étuve en tasse plastique*. Tours of the building will precede a car-boot sale of its furnishings, with special discounts to those shareholders who paid for them. There will be a short business session and a vote of thanks to the auditors. Later, at the Hammersmith Palais de Dance... No, sorry, correction, M. Attali seems to have sacked his spokesperson again, and these statements are inoperative. The meeting goes ahead as planned. The host government, with an apt sense of curiosity, is holding its party in the Natural History Museum, the Lord Mayor's is in Vintners Place, the Chancellor's banquet is in Merchant Taylors' Hall, and the president's banquet is *chez soi et chez son chef*. Oh, well, it may still work out cheaper to pour drinks down throats in London than to pour money down holes in eastern Europe. (24 April 1993)

The strange case of the World Bank and the six-legged yurts

I am worried about the World Bank. Change in what used to be the Soviet Union has overtaken us all, but the Bank has been sending teams to Kazakhstan to count six-legged yurts. All this started when Kazakhstan demerged itself and asked to join the Bank, becoming, a year ago, its 163rd member. The Bank's standard response to events is to commission a report. So it sent in two missions and has now published their findings in a fat red book with 41 joint authors. Its theme ('The government is on a risky path, yet the most critical risk is to waver') has the true non-executive ring of a leading article. Only those who read as far as the statistics will begin to boggle. They will find tables of Kazakhstan's imports and exports for its trade outside the Soviet Union. Linoleum contests the top spot for imports, sausage covers and restoration work are bottom of the league.

The export list is odder. Kazakhstan, as the report explains, is rich in oil and gas and gold but apparently cannot be bothered to sell them. Instead the list dribbles down through rugs and honey and egg powder to liquorice, sheep's innards, Alpine training arenas, beeswax and hooves. Then in last place come six-legged yurts. In 1990 they brought in 10,000 non-convertible roubles, failing in 1991 to repeat this modest score. I can only say that I am not surprised. A six-legged yurt, lord of the last frontier of zoology, Kazakhstan's answer to the pushmepullyu, must be worth a great deal of money or none at all. (9 October 1993)

Bridge finance

IMF meetings are unremittingly social ('How nice to see you again, Mr Cantquitereadyourbadge') and I vainly try to model my technique on Roy Bridge's. He was the pound's manager and wily defender – 'The Bank of England,' James Callaghan said of him, 'used to have a man who understood these things' – and much in demand for parties. 'Two things matter,' he explained to me. 'If you possibly can, keep one evening free. Otherwise, have a timetable and stick to it. For instance, I have to go to five parties this evening and must leave for the next one at 8.16.' He glanced at his watch like the White Rabbit. 'Good evening,' he said. And vanished. (8 October 1994)

Free trade, free tickets

Jobs and air tickets all round, boys – here comes the World Trade Organisation. It has agreed (first things first) to hold a jamboree in Singapore. In its fissiparous way it is giving birth to committees and councils, with plums for Japan and Sweden and Hungary and, as always, France, with Britain in its usual hopeless way left out. The top plum has yet to be picked, but Italy and Mexico (those economic success stories) have candidates. In Paris, Jean-Claude Paye is back in his otiose job at the Organisation for Economic Co-operation and Development, the club of developed countries which has just admitted Mexico. Some organisations are easier to start than to stop. (4 February 1995)

Rolling back the frontiers of the public sector – starting with ostriches

Ministries need ways of justifying their existence, so you will be pleased to learn that the Ministry of Agriculture, Fisheries and Food has an expert on ostriches. He is Nigel Church of ADAS, the Ministry's advisory service, and by his own account, what he does not know about ostriches would hardly fill an eggcup. He acts as a consultant to Her Majesty's Government, the European Union and the Food and Agriculture Organisation of the United Nations. All these bureaucracies need ostrich policies, or think they might, one day. Ostriches are the fad of the moment. Sure-fire schemes for investing in them flock in by every post, promising that my money will multiply even faster than the ostriches.

I would not bet on it. I seem to remember an angora goat scheme (it moulted). There was certainly a pig scheme that trailed one weary pig around the country, to be shown to a series of investors, each of whom was led to believe that he owned it. There are some good ostrich schemes, Mr Church says, and some very bad ones. He must be right, but there is a moral in this for a Prime Minister now suddenly intent on rolling back frontiers of the public sector. It can be done, he says. Jolly difficult, grumbles the Chancellor: people nowadays expect all sorts of services. I wonder. The two of them might start by cutting out or selling off the advisory service on ostriches. My advice is free: if you are tempted to buy an ostrich, put your head in the sand until the feeling goes away. (10 February 1996)

Laying an egg

Now that ostriches have written themselves into my Bad Investment Guide, I am reminded that the Lord gave Job an early warning: 'Gavest thou wings and feathers unto the ostrich? Which leaveth her eggs in the earth, and warmeth them in dust, and forgetteth that the foot may crush them, or that the wild beast may break them; because God hath deprived her of wisdom, neither hath He imparted to her understanding.' So much for the ostrich nest egg. (20 April 1996)

This week's good cause

Boondoggles like Unctad (United Nations Commission for Trade and Development) outlive their usefulness – those that ever had any – because they are easier to start than to stop. They are set up in a blaze of philanthropy. Then the empire builders move in, and white marble for their offices becomes the week's good cause. Then the next week's good cause is a job for some minister's western-educated second cousin. Then the ministers defend them and the cousins are all for expanding them. No one has an interest in shutting them, or no one but the taxpayers who inadvertently support them. So on they go, regardless of cost or point. Does Asia, the lair of the tiger economies, still need an Asian Development Bank? Does Vienna need a UN agency that promotes industrial development, in its own quiet way?

To the reformers – and Kenneth Clarke can sound like one – I suggest two rules of thumb. First, for every such agency created, another must be strangled. Second, every agency should have a self-destruct clause, which would wind it up on a fixed and not too distant date unless its sponsors positively vote to keep it going. Alternatively, they could spend the money on good causes. (17 February 1996)

A boondoggle is born

John Bruton was prime minister of Eire from 1994 to 1997.

Then felt I like some watcher of the skies when a new planet swims into his ken. Before my eyes, a boondoggle is being born. It has all that a boondoggle should have – air tickets to Bangkok and a cast of thousands, with everything laid on regardless (as with all good boondoggles) of cost or point. The Prime Minister will be present at the birth, and that nice Mr Bruton is flying out too, so Bangkok might be just the place to talk about Belfast.

What has lured them there is the Asia Europe Meeting. Nothing too specific about the agenda, of course. It will set goals for relationships – Bangkok is good at them. It will set Europe trading with Asia, something that would obviously never have occurred without a boondoggle to show the way. Will it reach any decisions? I can think of one. All present will agree that the meeting was most useful – so useful, in fact, that it must be a regular fixture, with the venues alternating: in Nice next year, perhaps, then Bali... For this it will need a well-paid secretariat, with even more air tickets – unless, that is, John Major stands up in Bangkok and says that the world has enough boondoggles, and enough boondogglers keeping them going at everyone else's expense, without conjuring up new ones. I fear that he is too polite. Next time he should send someone ruder. I could use the air ticket myself. (2 March 1996)

We'll meet again

The great Bangkok boondoggle ran absolutely true to form. It reached the decision I forecast a week ago: 'All present will agree that the meeting was most useful – so useful, in fact, that it must be a regular fixture, with the venues alternating.' The next Asia Europe Meeting will be held in London, and the one after that in Seoul, so boondogglers from east and west can start wangling their air tickets now. (9 March 1996)

Say we've lost the money, and go home – the world's debtors deserve better

The war in Vietnam was going badly wrong. What, asked the President, should the strategy be now? A hand shot up: 'Say we've won and go home.' This advice has now been taken by the World Bank, the International Monetary Fund and their richer members gathered here [*Washington*]. What were they to do about the world's most hopeless debtors? Answer: write off the debt and declare it a victory. The money, after all, is lost and gone forever, and all that remains is to put the best face on loss – to chalk it up to good works and the relief of necessity.

Now, the lenders should be asking what went wrong last time. They might then conclude that there was too much lending, and too much of it was badly conceived and badly managed. The World Bank, in particular, measured success as a development agency by the volume of money it could pump out. That was well meant, but the money found its way into projects which could never earn their keep and left nothing behind them but the scars of debt and the slag heaps of compound interest. Much of the lending went wrong for the simplest and saddest of reasons: rich people in poor countries pocketed the money. Now is the lenders' chance to make debt forgiveness conditional on honest and open government. It would be a pity to muff that chance. Rather late in the day, the World Bank is talking of the need to detect corruption and to stamp it out. I know just the man for this – an investigative accountant who was sent out by Shell to look for a fraud in Nigeria. He told me that it was like looking for a haystack in a needle. (5 October 1996)

Karki drill

I applaud the initiative of Kishun Dhoj Karki, who has smuggled himself and three kilograms of hashish into Australia by passing himself off as the finance minister of Nepal. This confirms my belief that many impostors now pose as finance ministers, and that they fly round the world to boondogglish meetings so that they can distribute opiates. Thus, in October last, 'Gordon Brown' did not fly to Hong Kong by way of Mondorf-les-Bains, Mauritius, Madagascar, Johannesburg and Bangkok. That was an impostor, and the real Mr Brown stayed at home with his feet up. He should stay there next week and avoid the impostors in Brussels who will purport to sign up for a single pseudo-currency. (25 April 1998)

All washed up

A big hand for the Republic of Palau, which this week becomes the IMF's 182nd and newest member. I cannot say where it is but my finger would be on the South Pacific. The last atoll to join from that part of the world, Micronesia I think, at once asked for a loan. This request went down badly. A loan? What do you think we are, the World Bank? What do you want a loan for, anyway? To build a wall, its finance minister suggested. This was even worse: the IMF was not engaged in project finance, and anyway, what did he want a wall for? Well, said the minister, if we don't build one round our country quickly, the sea will come in and the IMF will be one member short. (10 October 1998)

A warm, cosy glow

The Seattle meeting of the World Trade Organisation was intended to launch a bold 'Millennium' agenda for free trade, but ended in failure amid violent demonstrations.

How hurtful for President Clinton. He called a boondoggle and nobody came. Well, Rentaprotesta was well represented, but his fellow heads of state and government developed subsequent engagements and stayed at home. Seattle may have its attractions (such as the traffic lights programmed by Bill Gates when he was a lad), but it is a long way to go for the pleasure of sitting in on a meeting of the World Trade Organisation. They may also think that the WTO is degenerating into a conventional boon-doggle, looking after itself and busy with its own affairs, such as the struggle which only ended when the two claimants for the top job agreed to take it in turns.

If the meeting was meant to launch a new 'Seattle Round' of tariff cuts, do not expect to see this good ship whizzing down the slipway into Puget Sound. Free trade has lost some of its impetus, and the French (for example) are finding new ways to resist it. That is bad news for the world's poorest countries, which could feed the rest of us so much more cheaply if we had the grace to let them, and bad news for this country, which exports one third of all it produces and needs to find its markets open – but perhaps it will give the protesters a warm glow, which they will need in Seattle. (4 December 1999)

Turn-up for the book

The Grand International Boondoggle Handicap was a rough race in which the favourite was nobbled, prompting the stable to insist that its second string should be declared the winner. The prize is to be managing director of the International Monetary Fund (so what can the second prize be? The World Bank?) and Horst Köhler got there by being German. He may be better, all the same, than the form book suggests. I look forward to hearing him say that, like other monetary institutions, it should learn to manage with smaller offices and fewer people. The bankers have had to learn this already. One of them quoted Lloyd George on Bonar Law, the Conservatives' compromise choice as their leader: 'The damned fools have chosen the right man by accident.' (10 June 2000)

Swiss roll-up

We haven't had a good new three-ring boondoggle for quite a while, so I welcome the World Information Summit, which promises to be a classic. At least 56 heads of government are booked into Geneva next month, with the usual full supporting cast of ministers, bag carriers and freeloaders. What a boost for the lakeside economy! No wonder that the Swiss franc is so strong.

All that remains is to decide what the great men will talk about. Their sherpas have spent the last week on reconnaissance in Geneva, talking about talks, but have got nowhere. It occurs to me that they might submit proposals for a virtual information summit, in which the participants would stay at home and send each other e-mails – but that, of course, would miss the whole point, or lack of point, of a boondoggle. This one has already reached the decision that matters, which is where and when to meet next: in 2005 in Tunisia. Order your camel now and bill it to your taxpayer. (22 November 2003)

Consolation prize

The ashes of John Maynard Keynes were scattered on a Sussex hillside, which is all that now prevents him from turning in his grave. The International Monetary Fund, his invention, 60 this year, has become a consolation prize. The managing director's post is vacant, convention reserves it for a candidate from Europe, but Jean Lemierre is staying on at the European Boondoggle for Remuneration and Disbursement, so that only leaves – Wim Wimp? Jacques-Anonyme Enarque? Rodrigo Rato, known, if at all, as finance minister in a government thrown out a few weeks ago by the Spanish electorate?

Ooh, you guessed. Candidates should have been asked what they thought the IMF was for, now that Keynes's original hopes have flown out of the window. They would have been invited to parse its $300 billion balance sheet, and to comment on my first law of international finance: never lend to Argentina. (24 April 2004)

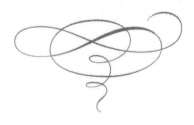

Open wide

When appointed to the European Commission, Edith Cresson arranged for it to give employment to her dentist.

As for jobbery and patronage, I dare say that Edith Cresson's favoured dentist knows just as much about youth, training and human resources as she does. The two of them just turn to the Commission's paymasters and say: open wide.

Patronage gave Edith Cresson her start, and her patron was François Mitterrand. Even then, her appointment caused comment. 'What an odd thing to do,' said Stani Yassukovich. 'You might give an old girlfriend a Cartier brooch, but you don't make her prime minister.' Or a European commissioner, either. Now her pay-off will be big enough to buy her something nice from Cartier. (20 March 1999)

PART II

SUBURBAN

CHAPTER SEVEN

DEAR OCCUPIER...

The perils of the housing market, and my plan to move into the Ritz

It is a deeply rooted national belief that we should all get rich by buying a brick box with borrowed money and then living in it. In the last two decades, we have seen two raging booms in house prices, and one bust. That chastening experience, I thought, might cure us of our fond delusion. How wrong I was – though when a room at the Ritz cost no more than the interest on a mortgage on a house in Fulham, the switch looked most attractive. As the boom roared on, I founded the Stopped Clocks Club and offered associate membership to the Bank of England, which shared my belief that this was too much of a good thing (or bad thing) to last. Even a stopped clock is right twice a day.

Down in the docks

I wondered how soon the first crack in the house market would follow the crack in the stock market. To complete the sale of its Hackney development, Pilot Properties is now offering 5 per cent price cuts. Good tactics – the first cuts are the best. Travelling, as I now find myself doing, between metropolitan London and the Isle of Dogs (or North Greenwich), I have time to observe all the new houses, old warehouses and riverside flats at various stages of readiness for the ever-expanding City population which was expected to flow out eastwards.

Certainly, the prospective owners had no trouble in financing their purchases. Some found it possible to borrow the full purchase price and, on top of that, enough money to service the loan for three years. They happily calculated that within the three years, house prices would have risen far enough to give them a free ride for the duration and a capital stake at the end of it. In some developments, sold off the drawing board, a secondary market has developed. The game is to put down a deposit on a flat, intending to sell it on before completion. Since the normal deposit is one-tenth of the full price, this is a market operating on 90 per cent margin. A great game, so long as the markets – in houses, shares, jobs, salaries and bonuses – were going upwards. It looks like a bruising game now that the music has stopped. (28 November 1987)

The seven year twitch

House prices go up in the same way that God pays – that is, not every Tuesday. Over time they have risen as people have become better able to afford their mortgage payments out of income, but not at the same pace, by any means. Last year the average house price rose to four and a half times the average income – the highest this ratio has ever been. Seven years ago and seven years before that, the ratio fell back, to three times. If that seven-year cycle comes round again, house prices will fall, as the

Bank of England predicts, and the only question will be how far.
(25 February 1989)

If mortgages didn't exist, nobody would be allowed to invent them

You signed what? An agreement to borrow money for 20 years? How much money? Dear me, that must be about four times what you earn in a year... Quite. And at what rate of interest? The man didn't say, except that it can go up and down? Up and down in line with what? In line with whatever the lender likes to make it? And what happens if you don't like it? Can you pay it back? Yes, I heard you – using what? I meant, do you have the option? The man said it was subject to penalty, the lender will demand more money from you if you try to pay him back? What size of penalty? Whatever the lender likes to say it is? You know, speaking as your adviser, I'd say that you're the sort of person who if he hasn't got his adviser with him shouldn't leave the house. By the way, have you given any security for this loan? Your house? Gosh. And what did the man call this? A mortgage? He says everybody has one? Oh, I see...

The great British mortgage, if it did not exist, would hardly be allowed to be invented. Lawyers would shake expensive heads at such unlimited risks, consumer councils would counsel avoidance, and building society managers would find cameramen on their doorsteps and feet in their doors. How have they, and we, been able to stay out of trouble all these years? We have been protected, without thinking about it, by three lines of defence, but one of them has gone and the other two will now be put to the test.

In the dozy old days when the building societies had the mortgage market to themselves, they set their interest rates, as you might expect, by cartel. Once a month they would all go to lunch at their Association, which would then 'recommend' a rate. Now the cartel has crumbled, and that line of defence has crumbled with it. The next line is the price of houses. So long as prices were rushing on upwards, neither the borrower nor the lender had too much to worry about. The borrower's capital gain more than made up for the cost of his financing. As for the lender, his market was growing prodigiously, and his security improving every day. (25 February 1989)

Squeaky girls and easy money – five years on, the house party is over

London house prices rose between 1980 and 1988 at a compound rate of 14.3 per cent a year. In some parts of the country house prices then fell by more than 20 per cent in less than two years from their peak in 1989.

It is five years since I met the squeaky girl with the refrigerator full of champagne. She was trying to sell me a house – or rather, in those heady days, telling me to buy it, at or above the asking price, before someone else did. I asked whether the champagne came with it. 'Oh, no,' she said, 'it's for all the other agents when we have the party to launch the house.' Now they have vanished – the champagne, the girl, the other agents and agencies, the easy money that surrounded them, and the great soaring bubble of house prices that carried them all up. Its bursting came as a shock, to ministers who counted on it to reward a property-owning democracy, to brokers and dealmakers and decorators and lawyers who lived by it, to lenders who have lost fortunes, and to borrowers who may have lost everything, including their houses.

In this column five years ago, I worried about what the squeaky girl and her friends were letting us in for. They had all been drawn in by the lure of a market which seemed to go only one way – upwards. Immediately, that was a self-fulfilling prophecy, as new lenders poured money in from every side and staid old bodies like the Prudential fell over their feet to buy house agents. They all had to try harder, which meant cutting margins, including the margins of safety. 'There is evidence' (I wrote) 'of lending against inflated values, with minimal checks, and below the cost of wholesale money in the City's markets.' It could not, I thought, be as easy as all that. Credit would be tightened up; lenders would burn their fingers and drop out; there would even be new competition for savings; even the house buyers' tax breaks might not be sacrosanct. If this were any other market, from government stocks to fish-meal futures, you could see that a correction was coming. This, though, was the house market, where prices had gone up, year in, year out, for a quarter of a century. Was it immune to the law of gravity? I did not think so. The house market bubbled on for another 18 months and when the Chancellor, Nigel Lawson, in his 1988 budget took two of its tax breaks away, buyers rushed to get houses and mortgages before the bar came down.

After that, gravity took over. A market which, having gone to a peak, then slips back by 15 or 20 per cent is only behaving as markets do. Stock markets can do it in a week. The house market has done that – and as for the borrowers, about 100,000 of them will lose their houses this year. (23 November 1991)

Gloom, Britannia

House owners are gloomier than they have ever been, or at least since the Britannia Building Society started asking them questions. They think that houses are good value, but more than half of them are not confident at all that prices will go up. I bet that if the Britannia had put the same questions seven years ago, it would have got the answers in reverse – houses are frightfully expensive, but prices are sure to go on rising, aren't they? No: that was the top.

Now all the money and confidence are in the stock market, which is reaching new heights, while house prices lag behind. Billion-pound takeover bids pour out cash, which must be reinvested. You might call that asset price inflation – in which case you would think it only a matter of time before it spread to houses. (26 August 1995)

Here come Rupert and Samantha again, giving me the feelbad factor

I suppose that the Blairs must be trading up. The Halifax Building Society says that Islington house prices have risen by 40 per cent. This is just like the old days when I bought a house there and was told that the neighbourhood was up-and-coming. So it was, in the sense that Brazil is the country of the future and always will be. Now it is with deepening depression that I hear the Ruperts and Samanthas, in the estate agencies and in Conservative Central Office, talking up a housing boom once more. Welcome back to the feelgood factor, they burble – prices will rise by a third by the end of the century, don't miss the boat...

It was not difficult to see that cheap money and cheap houses would suffice to turn the market round. House prices can go up as well as down. There was a time when people thought they always would go up and always should, so that we could all get rich by financing our biggest and our least productive assets with somebody else's money. The ruling party was not content that an Englishman's home would be his castle. It had to be his gold mine, too. It was exempted from the laws of economics. When the price of baked beans went up that was inflation, but when the price of houses went up that was prosperity.

At the peak of the market, first-time buyers were having to borrow 90p of each pound that they spent on their houses. The moment the market turned down, they were ruined. They and others learned the hard way what a dangerous illusion a housing boom can be, and it seems rather soon to forget. Indeed, in any market, fallen favourites never quite come back. (20 July 1996)

Wait for it, but the time will come to move out of houses and into the Ritz

I am getting ready to sell my house and move into the Ritz. No hurry, of course, but these things need planning and timing. If I get it right, I shall be rich – well, richer, anyhow. It would have worked last time round. For most of the 1980s the right thing to do was to be long of property and short of money. The rate of increase in house prices was higher than the rate of interest on mortgages, so, roughly speaking, the bigger your house was and the more money you borrowed against it, the richer you got. It paid us to run our net holdings of cash down to zero and even below.

Then, suddenly, the balance reversed. Interest rates soared, house prices tumbled, and it paid to be short of property and long of money, with your cash in the bank and yourself in a hotel room or a tent, preferably rented. Few of us timed that one right. Most of us were caught on the wrong foot and stayed there, watching impotently as our wealth diminished. In the end we were washed off the rocks by a flood tide coming in from the stock market. The stocks and shares we own, and those that the life assurance offices and pension funds own for us, came to be worth more than our stakes in our houses.

Now houses are catching up. Our personal wealth (which Michael Saunders of Salomon Smith Barney measures) has risen by 7 per cent in a year, after allowing for inflation, and the second quarter of this year saw the steepest jump since the 1980s. Once again house prices are leaving interest rates behind. If history repeats itself the stock market will crack before the house market does, so I have time in hand (and a signal to watch for) before I switch into the Ritz. On second thoughts, I might pay off my mortgage and stay put. Houses are for living in. (28 August 1999)

Putting on the Ritz

My plans to sell my house and move into the Ritz are beginning to take shape. Already the arithmetic looks good. I would like to think that, as a regular customer, I could reserve a room there for not too much more than £1000 a week. This would provide a roof over my head and cover any number of domestic costs – council tax, water rates, lighting and heating, housekeeping, linen, security, porterage and oil to pour into the bath and make bubbles. Breakfast in London's most beautiful dining room will probably be extra. Even so, at something like £60,000 a year my deal would compare very favourably with the cost of mortgaging a house in London.

The interest rate on a mortgage from the Halifax was until this week set at 6.85 per cent, and at that rate interest payments of £60,000 a year gross up to a capital sum of £876,000. Given the way that the London house market is going, that sort of money would scarcely buy you a pied-à-terre in Fulham. Just at the moment, of course, you might do better to borrow the money and move into Fulham, hoping that your house will increase in value by more than £60,000 a year. Deutsche Bank seems to think that prices are set to go up by a third. The art will be to time that move into the Ritz for the moment when the bubble bursts and prices start to fall. No bell will ring in the market to tell us when that moment comes. Book now. (11 September 1999)

To let, vacant

Buying to let is our latest idea of a painless way to make money – a worthy successor to investing in champagne for the millennium and joining Lloyd's of London. Now Savills, the estate agents, reckon that prime London rents have come down by 10 per cent, thanks to a rising supply of buy-to-let properties. Over the next two years, they expect more empty property and rents which are falling or static.

Nick Whitehouse has seen it before: 'First the insurance, then the annual maintenance charge, then the things that go wrong, before you even get to the tenant who leaves in the middle of the night with three months' rent unpaid, having painted the internal walls purple, orange and black. Finally the Bank of England decides that interest rates have to go up, so that your return is now negative. You get so fed up that you hand the keys back to the bank and write off your investment.' It then becomes the bank's worry and you are free to look round for another way to make money. (2 March 2002)

Flat out

High on the list of offers I can refuse is buying to let. Even before Cherie Blair bet £500,000 on a pair of flats in Bristol, sight unseen, I did not share her adviser's belief that this was a sure way to make money. This week Sir Howard Davies, chairman of the Financial Services Authority, ran up a storm signal. Borrowed money had flooded into buy-to-let schemes, he said: 'Rents have fallen in London for five successive quarters. Some borrowers are finding that rental incomes are not covering the cost of servicing the mortgage.' That would leave them to pin their faith on ever-rising prices – but if prices fell, they might not be able to pay their mortgages back. London prices are weakening. No doubt we shall be told that Bristol is quite different, but I would not bet on it. (15 February 2003)

Mervyn's mule

I was telling Mervyn King, the Governor of the Bank of England, that the way to catch a mule's attention was to hit it with a length of four by two planking. In the months that followed, he showed signs of taking my advice.

The party that still roars on is the great British house party. A boisterous few months have persuaded the Nationwide that house prices, this year, are on their way up by another 15 per cent. The faster they rise, the more we can and do borrow against them, spending the proceeds on riotous living or investing them in property, by putting down a 10 per cent deposit to make a quick turn on a newly built flat. I last saw this game played 15 years ago in Docklands. That was a red-hot market, and when it cooled down the depositors vanished. Today's market looks hot enough to be handled with oven gloves, and among the professionals I begin to notice signs of caution.

The Bank expects house prices to level out by the end of next year. It has been expecting this, on and off, for some years now; I have been expecting it for even longer, and shall only add now that, every so often, a stopped clock turns out to be right. The Chancellor has left the costs of housing out of his new index, shamelessly preferring not to count them as inflation, and expecting the monetary policy committee to take this at its face value. When something looks like a mule, reacts like a mule and is as stubborn as a mule, it is probably a mule, and needs to be hit on the head. (15 February 2003)

"When the price of baked beans went up that was inflation, but when the price of houses went up that was prosperity.**"**

CHAPTER EIGHT

I. K. GRICER'S RAILWAY JOTTINGS

A Platonic view of civilised travel as it is and as it might be

Railways are the the conjunction between City and Suburban. The Lord Mayor can wake up in the Mansion House and walk downstairs to work, but he is the exception. No wonder the City has a love–hate relationship with the railways, a state of mind familiar to my railway correspondent, I. K. Gricer. He shares my own belief in a Platonic ideal, sometimes discernible in maps and timetables and archives, to which actual railways might imperfectly conform. Disparities between the ideal and the real become apparent. In our years together we have been shunted, derailed and rerouted, just like the railways themselves, but we chuff on. I suspect that Gricer's ideal was built to a broad gauge, for steam traction.

❝Readers sometimes inquire about my correspondent's unusual name. Can he, they ask me, be one of the Somerset Gricers? It is perhaps not surprising that an apprentice at Swindon in the glorious twilight of steam should have been christened Isambard Kingdom, but light on his surname appears to be cast by the Wordsworth Railway Dictionary: 'Gricer: the most fanatical and extreme type of railway enthusiast, intent on travelling over all existing railway track, seeing all existing locos etc. Often used in a derogatory sense. Origins obscure.' The verb 'to grice' is a back-formation. When I put this to my correspondent, he says that it is just a coincidence. **❞**

Gibbs G.W.R.

May I be the first to wish City and Suburban readers a very happy sesquicentenary of the Great Western Railway. That masterpiece on rails (and quite respectable investment) dates from 1835, so that this new year will resound with commemorative whistling and hooting. There must be a place for the great banking family of Gibbs, who promoted it. They are still scattered across the City, though their bank has now been swallowed up by the Hongkong and Shanghai. In 1835 there were Gibbses on both the committees (Bristol and London) which brought the railway into being, and it was in the Fenchurch Street offices of Antony Gibbs's bank that some unknown director left a mightier name than his own behind him. He opposed the original, uninspired plan to name the railway London & Bristol: 'Call it Great Western,' he said. (5 January 1985)

Missing the boat

British Rail's high-speed link is now in action, stretching for some 15 miles across rich countryside, carrying trains at 125 mph and engineered for higher speed. This is the new stretch of the East Coast Main Line, built to bypass the curves and subsidence at Selby, and it bears out my theory that the way to link British Rail to the Channel Tunnel is to stick a pin in the middle of England and whirl it around. We have fine fast trains, but none of them runs south from London. The first morning train to Dover covers the 77 miles in two hours. It would be quicker to go to Taunton, Cardiff, Crewe, Leeds or York (188 miles). If any serious attempt had been made to bring the boat train routes up to the standards now familiar on other lines, the railways and their minister would not be in their present pickle. (23 June 1990)

Arnold of Runcorn

If you are thinking of ringing up Runcorn railway station, don't ask for the number. It's gone ex-directory. The patient people at directory inquiries tell me that this is British Rail's new policy: no numbers to be given for stations. All callers to be referred to the number for passenger train inquiries, whether they need it or not. This is the sort of bright idea that British Rail, so Keith Waterhouse tells us, gets from its brother-in-law Arnold – or from the gas boards, with their ex-directory showrooms, where the staff were safe from any tiresome calls from customers. Dear Runcorn station, if you still take deliveries of racing pigeons, I could send you one, with a message. (27 February 1993)

Backing up

Limerick Junction was so designed that all trains from all directions had to come in backwards. The Listowel and Ballybunion was a monorail, with drawbridges for level crossings. At Ballina the branch line was powered by a horse which was frightened of steam engines. To John Prideaux, historian of Irish railways and manager of British railways, these arrangements must now seem relatively sensible. Having distinguished himself by bringing the Inter-City services into profit, he was put in charge of a string of dots on the map and briefed to turn it into a fast line from London to the Channel Tunnel. He redrew it as a new main line for Kent, moved the dots, bagged St Pancras for his terminus, saved billions on the estimates – and has now been derailed and taken out of service, as the latest victim of violent, conflicting movements on the railways. (28 August 1993)

Off the rails and in the dark

The people of Kent appear to be frightened of trains. Perhaps they have not noticed any lately. I can see how it happens. Crossing their county the other evening, I found it festooned with motorways – wide, noisy, brilliantly lit and in the process of being made bigger. Every so often I would traverse a dark, narrow, silent trough, with a single green light in the distance. These were railway cuttings. The idea that the county might get another railway, towards the end of this century, has come as a terrible shock. The plans for the Channel Tunnel link line are still not complete, but I have two suggestions for speeding things up. First, show the protestors what a modern railway (the East Coast main line, for example) is like. Second, make some of the trains stop for them. (29 January 1994)

Off the rails

I could see what was wrong with the railways' finances when I met their missing customer. She was a director who, based in London, commuted to Warrington. Using the West Coast main line, I asked her? Not a bit of it – driving up and down to get the business mileage for her car. That should send the men in white coats hurrying round to the Treasury, which must be suffering from fiscal dementia as well as rising damp. The Chancellor now hopes to sell the main line itself, as an asset in Railtrack. Then he hopes to sell a franchise to run trains on it. Then he hopes to raise private-sector finance to improve it. Then he gives a first-class customer a tax incentive not to use its fast and comfortable services but to wear out the M1 and M6 by slogging up and down them in the sleet. Barking. (11 February 1995)

Digging yourself into a hole

To Brunel or Stephenson, digging the hole was the hard bit. Your navvies hacked and blasted their way through the Box escarpment or the Kilsby ridge until at last they saw daylight. Then you put rails down and ran trains on them. That was the easy bit. Since those heroic days it has become more difficult, driving Sir Alastair Morton to impotent fury. His navvies hacked and blasted their way beneath the Channel and dug him a beautiful hole, all ready for the trains…

Trains? What trains? You want them to start right away? Be reasonable, guv, they changed the specifications and we can't get the parts. The first ones will be coming along in the new year. Mark you, with this new technology, they'll need to be run in and you must expect teething troubles. Wossat? What was wrong with the old technology? You know how it is, guv, the boys must have their toys. Besides, we get so held up with Common Market regulations, you wouldn't believe. Still, I suppose that's progress, innit? Honest, if I was you, I wouldn't have told the punters they could turn up and drive on. Not in Land-Rovers, anyhow. Look at those geezers, haven't they heard of waiting their turn? Tell them the service has been delayed due to unforeseen circumstances. Tell 'em there's fish on the line. They're your bankers? Tough on them.

By this time Sir Alastair's eyes are going round like pinwheels. Bankers do not wait before they charge interest, and by the end of last year Eurotunnel owed them £8 billion. His job is to make its revenues run fast enough to catch up with its interest bill. When Eurotunnel tapped its shareholders for money, a year ago, that crossover point was pencilled in for 1998, but the forecasts in that prospectus have been missed. The bankers have been given a year's start, and their bill is compounding and accelerating. We are not going bust, says Sir Alastair. (15 April 1995)

Gricer on the Jubilee

I. K. Gricer is blowing off steam. His latest proposal is to merge the Channel Tunnel rail link with the Jubilee Line extension. Like that, he says, we should dig only one expensive and otiose railway tunnel under East London, and not two. Offering those who are bored with the Central Line's scenery a longer route from Stratford-atte-Bow to Bond Street, this extension was due to open some years ago but is, of course, running over time and over budget. Announcing the latest delay, London Underground now plans to open in the spring of 1999 and seems to have dropped the idea that passengers should make part of the journey on foot. Meanwhile the work continues to absorb the capital investment needed on those parts of the Underground network where the trains, when not frozen into place by signal failures, run. Such are the hazards of financing public-sector projects. The Treasury thanks the shade of Gladstone (its tutelary deity) that the rail link is not one of them. (14 February 1998)

Hitting the buffers

One of the factors driving the soaring stock market was talk of a digital 'information superhighway'.

We have been here before. A new superhighway, a revolution in communications, a runaway market, new investors piling in – we saw them a century and a half ago with the great railway boom, and what a thump there was when they hit the buffers! From those days there survives a report of the Hum and Diddlesex Railway Company's meeting: 'They had lately opened six miles of the Navvy and Stoker Extension Branch, which he had no doubt would pay well when a town had arisen at each end and traffic was induced between them. (A voice: What's the expense?) The chairman begged not to be interrupted. The board had recommended a net dividend of 10 per cent on the deficit, and this, after paying the directors' salaries, which, he was glad to say, had been raised £500 each per annum, would render it necessary for the shareholders at once to pay up the late £20 call. (Sensation.)' When it was all over, the *Railway Gazette* blamed the market: 'The men who perverted the systems of business so as openly to rig bubble schemes, concocted to rob the public, up to bubble premiums, ought to be reached by our criminal law or expelled from the Stock Exchange.' The moral is that you can take an iron horse to a superhighway but it may still be a non-starter. (30 January 1999)

Squaring the Circle

I. K. Gricer steams in with the latest from John Prescott under one arm and, in his other hand, his treasured copy of the Great Western Railway timetable for January 1902. The Prescott plan is to run trains off the main lines on to London Underground, and so to provide through services across London, and he has, of course, been told on all sides that it cannot be done. Gricer says that God's Wonderful Railway could do it at the beginning of the century. It ran through trains to the City from Windsor (via Baker Street) and from Reading (via Willesden Junction). It could fit its trains into what is now the Circle Line without disturbing the services which, so the timetable assures us, ran every few minutes. Mr Prescott will have noticed that the Circle Line now does not run at all. He should conjure up the spirit of J. L. Wilkinson, who ran the Great Western at the time, and encourage him to sort things out. Wilkinson has a walk-on part in Gricer's epic work, 'The Poppet Valves of George Jackson Churchward'. (26 June 1999)

Down the Tube

My railway correspondent has been shunted. Taking up Mr Prescott's plans to run main-line trains across London by way of the Underground, I. K. Gricer boasted that in 1902 the Great Western ran a train from Windsor to the City, over what used to be the Circle Line before it gave up. Why stop there, though? The London, Tilbury and Southend ran a train from Ealing all the way to Shoeburyness. Driver James Snelling (retired from the LT & S) points it out to me in the 1922 Bradshaw. It dives into the Underground at the west end of the system, as he says, makes its City stop at Mark Lane (now called Tower Hill) and charges on to Barking, where it discards the Underground's electric locomotives and is steam-hauled for the rest of the way. I count on Sir Alastair Morton at the new

Strategic Rail Authority to reinstate it. Where there's a will there's a railway. (17 July 1999)

I get up steam

One in the eye for my railway correspondent, I. K. Gricer. I was invited (or I opened his invitation) to officiate at the opening of the Kent and East Sussex Railway's extension to Bodiam. Whistles blew, bands played, biplanes flew low in salute, and I urged this splendid railway to engineer its way out to the main line and run its Pullman service to and through the Channel Tunnel. Now I. K. Gricer and I hope that the Kent and East Sussex will join us in our bid for the Isle of Wight railway franchise. We plan steam-hauled boat trains, offering fish suppers, with brill or bream scooped up from the water troughs and boiled in the boilers. (8 April 2000)

We regret the delay to the modern railway's arrival. This is due to second-guessing

Gerard Fiennes was the railwayman who announced at King's Cross: 'We regret the delay to the Yorkshire Pullman. It was due to bad management.' In the end his career ran into the buffers, when his book, *I Tried to Run a Railway*, went down badly with his masters. It was, he said, in part about what happened when non-railwaymen tried. Railways, he thought, needed running. He cited a district superintendent who watched the expresses from the refreshment-room door, with a pint in his hand, and put his success down to constant personal supervision. What they do not need is to be dug up all the time and replanted: 'When you reorganise, you bleed. Punctuality goes to hell. Safety starts to slip. Don't reorganise. Don't. Don't. Don't' – and don't, he adds, hire very top brass who know little about railways but a lot about organisation. That is a sure way to end up knee-deep in consultants, which is what happened to British Airways and to Marks

& Spencer. No wonder Gerry Fiennes complained of being second-guessed by British Railways' board. (25 November 2000)

Crossed rails

My railway correspondent, I. K. Gricer, is evading the call to become chairman of Railtrack, but from a buffet car near Crewe he breaks cover to draw my attention to Crossrail. This plan to run mainline trains east and west across London in tunnels is back on the wish list, blessed by Sir Alastair Morton at the Strategic Rail Authority. The Corporation of London loves and longs for it, my correspondent says, but the Treasury hates it. Last time round, the Treasury decided to economise on stations and got the interchange at Farringdon cut out. This wrecked the traffic projections, so Crossrail was spiked. Better luck this time, says I. K. Gricer. (17 February 2001)

Project Dyno-Rod

My correspondent's restless mind has moved on to the Post Office's underground railway. This runs from east to west across London, carrying letters, but its future is said be under review, which is taken to mean that it does not have one. I expect that a preservation society is already forming, but I. K. Gricer's ideas have gone further. This line, he says, should be relabelled Crossrail. Then, to whizz from the City to Paddington, we need only buy a first-class stamp and climb on board. Some of us might have to squeeze to fit into a narrow-gauge railway engineered for mailbags, but the Circle Line has its discomforts, too, and the Gricer project certainly beats pretending to build a standard-gauge Crossrail, one of these days, with let's-pretend private finance.

We could also undertake Project Dyno-Rod, my long cherished plan for the Waterloo & City Line, or Drain. This features anti-macassars and champagne (in Partner Class) and a train set so simple that we could rely on it, day in, day out. (16 November 2002)

BreakRail

I. K. Gricer has been munching his way round the system and reports serious discrepancies. On the East Coast Main Line, he reports, GNER upholds railway tradition by offering breakfast to all its passengers, serving it on good china and glass with the company's crest and presenting a suitable bill. Breakfast on Virgin's West Coast Main Line is for first-class passengers only, and the price is lumped into the fare, which is loaded, as they have to be. They get no refund when breakfast is cancelled owing to a signal failure in the Watford area. Some Great Western trains now boast travelling chefs, but it is no use asking them for Churchillian breakfasts of kedgeree, cold grouse and burgundy. They can run to a breakfast baguette, which, in first class, arrives on a plate. On the Southern Railway's Brighton Belle, the kippers were favoured by Laurence Olivier, but breakfast on the Southern now appears to be extinct. My correspondent expects an early initiative from Stephen Byers, complete with elastic statistics, rapid reversals, fortuitous funerals, travelling lawyers and (just what the railways need) another regulator, to be called Offbreak, or BreakRail. (30 March 2002)

Claudine's golden age

Old British Rail hands will have happy memories of Claudine's, the massage parlour on the ground floor of BR's Euston Road head office. Somehow, Claudine's escaped privatisation, and thus earned its place in Terry Gourvish's history of the state-owned railway, now completed in a second massive volume. (10 August 2002)

The longest mushroom farm

My railway correspondent, I. K. Gricer, wants to know what to do about his shares in Eurotunnel. He bought them when they came to market, attracted by the prospect of free travel, but failing to spot that in order to qualify he had to turn up in a car. Since then the shares have lost most of their value, and at the annual meeting next week a band of rebels will propose to oust the board. Hostile circulars and counter-circulars ('this great project has become a nightmare', 'vulgar and personal... who are these men?') have whizzed between the battle lines. The rebels seem to hope that governments will bail the project out – 'managing the political issues', they call this – and hint at a stand-off with Eurotunnel's banks.

The catch is that if Eurotunnel defaults, the banks are entitled to take over, running the business for themselves until they get their money back. The board has an ambitious plan called Project Galaxie, which would involve merging Eurotunnel with its rail links. This is at least directed to the project's basic troubles: a high superstructure of debt on a rickety capital base, and traffic that still falls far short of capacity. I have advised I. K. Gricer to vote with the board. This will not make him rich (and the banks, too, must suffer) but is better than the only credible alternative, a shareholding in the world's longest submarine mushroom farm. (3 April 2004)

Under water

The *coup d'état* at Eurotunnel, where a mob of French revolutionaries defenestrated the board, will have sent well-earned shivers down the spines of overpaid directors everywhere. How the new board intends to get out of its 31-mile long hole is quite another question. It plans to recruit highly qualified members from this side of the Channel, and my railway correspondent, I. K. Gricer, will await the call.

The Gricer plan, I can reveal, is to shore up the company's capital base by issuing a new class of shares, which will qualify for dividends to be paid in tickets. These would entitle the holders to whizz to and fro. The marginal cost would be minimal. For this project the costs that matter are what are rightly called sunk costs, which can only begin to be covered as the tunnel becomes more intensively used. I fear, though, that this coup has brought forward the date when Eurotunnel's bankers exercise their right to put the shareholders to sleep, dispense with the directors, and run the business for themselves. They will then have to decide whether they would get their money back more quickly by operating their tunnel as a transport artery or as a mushroom farm. (17 April 2004)

For this sort of money, we could have built a whole new railway

My railway correspondent, I. K. Gricer, is a public interest director of Network Rail, along with 99 others, and he tells me that at least one of its targets is sure to be hit. It was told not to make a profit, and it hasn't. Only an unwritten guarantee from Gordon Brown – off the public balance sheet, of course – can keep it going.

Rebuilding the West Coast Main Line ruined Railtrack and has become more expensive still under its public-interest successor. First budgeted at £2 billion, this project will certainly run into 11 figures and the search is on for scapegoats. The London and North Western Railway gets blamed for the earthworks it built a century ago to accommodate an extra pair of tracks. Robert Stephenson gets blamed for laying out a railway that was evenly graded but bendy. A high-tech signalling system would have let the Pendolino tilting trains whiz along at 140 mph if only it could have been made to work. (The Stephensons could make things work.)

Now these trains will run at 125 mph, which on the main lines out of King's Cross and Paddington has been standard practice for a generation. For this sort of money we could have had a new railway. Indeed, for two-thirds as much money a new railway from Folkestone to St Pancras is coming in on time and within budget: top speed, 186 mph. These projects are not too big to be managed. Oh, well, I. K. Gricer says that his train to Euston came in 13 min-

utes early, so we must be getting somewhere, however expensively.
(10 April 2004)

"As W. S. Gilbert wrote to the directors of the Metropolitan
Railway, 'Saturday mornings, though occurring at frequent
and well-regulated intervals, always seem to take this
railway by surprise.'**"**

CHAPTER NINE

CAPTAIN THREADNEEDLE REPORTS

My correspondent keeps an eye on the City's favourite sport

People in the City live by making books and taking prices, so it is not surprising that Captain Threadneedle, my racing correspondent, feels at home there. He claims to have served with the Bank of England Volunteers – motto 'No advance without security' – but since they were stood down after the Peninsular War, he may be boasting. Certainly he possesses the quality, essential in financial markets, of knowing that 15 to 8 is a better price than 7 to 4 without having to look it up. His friends in the City can still wear their top hats to Ascot, but City and Suburban Day at Epsom is not all it used to be.

City and Suburban

The City and Suburban ought, with a name like that, to have survived from the Victorian railways – compounded, like the North London line, of dusty carriages, undiscovered stations and fading memories of murders long ago. It is indeed a Victorian survival, but in racing – still drawing the bank holiday crowds to Epsom. There is also the Great Metropolitan, where the runners begin by passing the winning post in the wrong direction. City and suburban sportsmen will nowadays know how it feels. (9 June 1984)

Backing Mister Lawson

My racing adviser Captain Threadneedle has put me on to a horse called Mister Lawson. This spirited performer has won several races this season – though when at the Captain's suggestion I backed him to get me out of trouble at York, he appeared to feel that restraint was now called for and finished out of the money. I was curious to know why Mister Lawson (described in *Timeform* as spare and unfurnished-looking) was so named. The Captain draws my attention to the breeding – by Blushing Scribe, out of Nonpareil. (27 August 1988)

Tip for the Captain

Captain Threadneedle asks me to help out the Jockey Club, which needs a business sponsor for its Newmarket classics. At Epsom, Hanson sponsors the Derby and Oaks. Newmarket has until now relied on the support of General Accident, which, all too well-named, has dropped out. Where (asks the Captain) should the Club, in these hard times, turn now? I have a nap selection for him. Racing and drinking, as I need not remind him, go together. Whitbread and Hennessy have stamped their names on fine races and at Newmarket a unique opportunity presents itself. I look forward to the Two Thousand

(and One Thousand) Guinness. The trophies, as usual, would be optional. (11 July 1992)

Non-starter

The Grand National of 1993 had been reduced to a farce as a result of a false start and had to be rerun at a later date.

My racing correspondent, Captain Threadneedle, writes: It is many years since, in these columns, I likened the grandstand at Aintree to a derelict Cunarder slowly sinking in an overgrown goods yard. In those days the course was under an idiosyncratic form of one-woman management, and I never thought that I should feel nostalgic for her. Come back, Mrs Topham, almost all is forgiven. (10 April 1993)

In the saddle

The Ebor meeting at York is buzzing with reports of a blonde in foal to Lester Piggott. Students of bloodstock note that the great jockey comes from a famous racing family, and can trace his pedigree back through the Rickabies, Piggotts and Cannons to Honest John Day of Danebury, who trained for Lord George Bentinck ('The Derby? It is the blue ribbon of the turf'). They contrast him with the classic winner Zafonic, who, after an unsatisfactory race at Goodwood, has now retired to stud at the age of three.

Why, they ask, should Lester, who is 55 years older, still have to be out on the racecourse in all weathers? Horses should work harder for longer, and jockeys should be passing on their qualities to future generations. Proposals for syndicating their services are being discussed in York's champagne bar, though in Lester's case the money would obviously have to be right. (21 August 1993)

O Captain, my Captain!

Captain Threadneedle is to receive the singular honour of having a race named after him. So he joins racing's pantheon. The Derby, the St Leger, the Queen Mother Champion Steeplechase, the Captain Threadneedle Selling Hurdle... They will jump off over two miles at Huntingdon on 23 November, which is the Daily Telegraph Peterborough Chase Day, and the Captain will be on the course, striding out well. Racegoing readers will recognise his weathered trilby, sometime the property of Captain Ryan Price, the trainer – a brother officer, as Threadneedle likes to suggest – with its irregular contour corresponding to the upper cranial limit of hair. (30 October 1993)

Nap selection

Tip for Budget day from Huntingdon, where Captain Threadneedle's race was won in style by Tax the Devil. The Chancellor may be relieved to hear that Chiltern Hundreds finished nowhere. (27 November 1993)

National champion

Neville Crump, who has taken his last fence, was the first and only Balliol man to have trained a Grand National winner – three of them, in fact. This distinction was rather lost on Sir Edward Heath when the two of them met at a college reunion. Opening the conversation cautiously, Sir Edward asked: 'And who was your tutor?' 'Good God,' said the great man, 'I don't know. I can't even remember the names of my owners.' (25 January 1997)

The Captain and I are under starter's to gee up the Old Nanny Goat

Captain Threadneedle and I are reviewing our options. We had intended to bid for the Tote. Only days ago we were given the go-ahead by the Sunday Leaks division of the Labour

Party. New Labour, said the leaksman, was going to need all the money it could get, and £500 million from selling off the Tote would come in handy, so this would be its very first privatisation. The state might not actually own the Tote (which seems to own itself), but trivial objections like that had never stopped the Thatcher government from selling off the TSB. Now was our chance.

What the Tote needs, we shall say, is distribution. It still relies on selling tickets on the course and through its 216 betting shops in just the same way the banks used to rely on their branches to defend their position in the High Street. They, and the insurers too, have discovered that the High Street can be bypassed. Good systems linked up to an ordinary telephone wire can do wonders. Armed with nothing more, a bank made itself the market leader in motor insurance, and the Prudential is setting out to be a bank. The Tote could move beyond the High Street if only it had the systems to support real-time betting with a link to the customers' cash. The banks have the systems, hold the cash balances and are in the credit business too.

Our plan would put the Tote and the banks into partnership. We would invite them to tender. Together they could offer direct-debit betting, press-button betting, plastic betting, bets on overdraft – not just to a few smoky shops but to millions of homes where the punters have settled down to watch the racing. The Old Nanny Goat would be a kid again and pay a jackpot, and racing would be the winner – together, of course, with the Captain and me. (22 February 1997)

Cheltenham bumper

Captain Threadneedle and I have got our eyes on Gordon Brown. If he becomes Chancellor, he says, he will move the Budget back to March. [He did.] Racegoers now limbering up for an arduous three days at Cheltenham should be aware of the threat. Chancellors used to be foolish enough to bring in their budgets on Champion Hurdle days, and the Captain and I fought a long campaign against it. I would attend Nigel Lawson's briefings in a country suit and brown felt hat, and leave early, for Paddington. A physiotherapist was suborned to jab her thumbs into the Permanent Secretary to the Treasury and enlist him in our cause by force. Finally, the Chancellor (the previous Chancellor, that is) took the point and moved the Budget to November. It was a reform for which his name would deserve to be remembered. Don't let Labour ruin it. (8 March 1997)

It's the big race to run British racing and the Captain's under starter's orders

A turn-up for the books in the race for the top job in racing: Captain Threadneedle has thrown his hat into the silver ring. When the runners come under orders next week, the Captain will be there, facing the tapes. At stake is the chair of the British Horseracing Board, racing's governing body – vacant since early this year, when Lord Wakeham resigned, accusing his colleagues of crass stupidity. His successor must settle this turf war and work out who will pay for racing and how.

The Captain's manifesto, I can disclose, is revolutionary. He says that racing is in danger of becoming a museum, where (as John Connally said of the International Monetary Fund) everything that is not already stuffed ought to be. It has followed the same course round the same courses for a century. Such investment as it gets is scattered even-handedly. Two firms of overpriced caterers have long since had it carved up. (Last week's sponsors at Newmarket caused a sensation by insisting on bringing in a newcomer called Rhubarb, at least for themselves and their guests.)

Racing, the Captain says, is an industry run for itself – which is apt to prove fatal. It must learn to back its winners and to let its losers go. It should concentrate its investment and use it intensively, and not just for a few days a year. It should be building new courses on greenfield sites with good access, and allowing tired old courses to trade their fixture lists in. Customers' habits have changed in the course of the century, and the supermarket chains have noticed that, even if racing has not. The manifesto even quotes Lord Wakeham: a good dose of market forces would make a difference to racing. This kind of thing will have Captain Threadneedle cut in his club. (9 May 1998)

Bumping and boring

My specialist correspondents, I. K. Gricer (railways) and Captain Threadneedle (racing), are at loggerheads. The Captain began it, complaining that when he set off for Newmarket for the 2000 Guineas, the first classic of the season, he expected a race train but found himself crammed into a self-propelling tram-car, which apparently pottered out of Cambridge station at two-hourly intervals. Gricer asked him what else he expected from a tramline like the old Great Eastern but a tram, and urged him to abandon Newmarket in favour of Newbury or Newton Abbot, racecourses served by God's Wonderful Railway. The Captain then lodged an objection for bumping and boring, and Gricer reported him to Her Majesty's inspecting officers of railways. This is getting serious. If racing and the railways cannot pull their act together, I may have to start writing this column myself. (8 May 1999)

Place your bets

Two racehorse owners whose names are new to me write to me out of the blue ('Dear Sir, It has come to our attention through a high-quality database...') inviting me to bet for them. 'We are seeking persons of the highest integrity with a good solid financial background to assist us in placing OUR MONEY. An interest in horse-racing is not essential.' Commission on winnings. If this letter came to me from Nigeria I would know what to make of it. My racing correspondent, Captain Threadneedle, has recommended a gnomic reply: Any to come – gratefully accepted. (19 January 2002)

Moving story

Top story in the *Financial Times*: 'Tony Blair moved quickly yesterday.' Aha, says Captain Threadneedle, my racing correspondent; he must have got over his setback in training, he seems to be striding out well. I have to explain that the phrase has acquired a new meaning. 'Move to' is spin talk for wishful thinking in action. Thus, ministers move to distance themselves from allegations of cronyism. Companies move to play down reports of feuding in their boardrooms. Downing Street moves to reassert control of the agenda, and inconvenient realities are moved away. The FT's faithful message was that the Prime Minister would sell the European constitution to the voters. He would, of course, first have to move us to buy it. (26 June 2004)

Course work

Once I had opted to spend last week on a course, Ascot was plainly the course to be on. Captain Threadneedle marked my card. Extending the Royal meeting to a fifth day represented a severe test of stamina, he says, but class triumphed, as it will. If the Queen can stay the distance, so can the rest of us. The next test for her advisers is to decide where to take the meeting when the builders are in at Ascot, and my correspondent's money is on York. It is not for me to suggest how she might be accommodated, but her great-great-grandmother's very comfortable train (or so my railway correspondent, I. K. Gricer, tells me) is housed in the National Railway Museum, an easy canter from the course. (28 June 2003)

Yorker for Ascot

One up for Captain Threadneedle. The next test for the Queen's advisers, he reported from Ascot, was to decide where to take the Royal meeting when the builders were in, and his money was on York – now confirmed as the winner. The trouble at Ascot, he says, is the tunnel. Never the course's best feature and no better for its tiles and traffic lights, it was built by the sixteenth Duke of Norfolk so that ordinary racegoers could reach the paddock from the grandstand without having to pollute the Royal Enclosure. It is now time expired and will have to be excavated, before some hapless punter finds that first the roof and then the Queen falls in on top of him. No risk of that at York. (16 August 2003)

"The race is not always to the swift, nor the battle to the strong; though, as Runyon added, that is the way they are betting. **"**

CHAPTER TEN

LUNCH AT THE DEALMAKERS' ARMS

I say, waiter, put this hotel on the bill

The wild frontier between money and politics runs north and south through the Savoy Grill. Here, on neutral ground, the two sides could meet and exchange signals over lunch. It was always a favourite of the great City fixers; I called it the Dealmakers' Arms and the nickname stuck. Some of their most protracted battles were fought on this ground, with the Savoy itself as the prize. The result was symbolic: the new owners, venture capitalists from New York, had no time for the old guard or their tastes, which found refuge at the Ritz or Wiltons. As for the Grill's silver-topped carving trolley, it has found a good home at my club. Some of us still understand the importance of lunch.

Putting on the Ritz

There is jam for the lawyers' tea at the Ritz. They can thank the Fayed brothers, now taking over House of Fraser. The brothers already own the Ritz in Paris and claim to have covered the purchase price from a year's revenue in licensing out the name. They would hope to follow up with House of Fraser's best name, Harrods. Now, though, they are busily tangling with Revlon over the brand name Charles of the Ritz. Their lawyers have crossed the Atlantic, to pursue the world's biggest biscuit company (Ritz crackers) and a major tobacco company (Ritz cigarettes). They have enjoined our own dear Ritz Hotel not to market its Ritz champagne in France – something which was not actually at the top of its action list.

But whose is the name? London's Ritz maintains that it has the unfettered right to its name, is not beholden to its namesake in Paris and will rebuff (has, I gather, already rebuffed) any attempt to make it pay royalties. Indeed, it is going in for some licensing on its own account. (I wish it well, in the hope that somebody else's biscuits – or cigarettes or scent – may help to subsidise my own refreshments.) But in my mind's ear I can already hear the cackle of lawyers' letters. The Ritz's parent company, Trafalgar House, also owns the liner *Queen Elizabeth II*, and last year opened (under licence, I assume) a new shipboard shop – Harrods. (30 March 1985)

Inns of Court

Who owns the rights to the Ritz? The Fayed brothers, owners of the Paris Ritz and now of Harrods, are busily pursuing their claims against American multinational companies with Ritz brand names (City and Suburban, last week). Trafalgar House, owner of the London Ritz, is standing its ground. The immortal Cesar Ritz founded not one hotel but three – in Paris, London and Madrid. The English courts laid down in the 1920s that no ownership subsists in the bare word Ritz and its ritzy derivatives. The Florence Ritz, whose greatest asset must be its name, may have a nasty shock coming. The Ritz of the Skies is the head-in-air slogan of New Zealand's airline. The Gossard Ritz, part of the Courtaulds empire, is a brassière... Here are the signs of a rich vein of litigation – whence the idea that one of the warring Ritz groups will call its next hotel Weshallnothesitatetoissue Ritz. (6 April 1985)

Siege rations

The besieging hordes of Lord Forte's army are beginning to rattle the defenders in the Savoy camp. So I inferred when lunching in that camp's venerable bastion, Simpson's in the Strand ('When are we going to let women in? When we get nicked, sir.') To my table was brought a dish which elsewhere would be in the forefront of the new cookery: baked treacle roll and sauce béarnaise. I wonder who got the well-done rump steak and custard. (26 March 1988)

Noblesse oblige

Sir Hugh Wontner had been the long-serving chairman of the Savoy Group.

Rocco Forte has found something else to dislike in Sir Hugh Wontner: 'He started without a penny and now owns two country estates.' The Honourable Rocco, hereditary chairman of his public company, was of course born to the purple of commerce, but could surely afford to show condescension to those who rise from the ranks. (2 July 1988)

The Caz canteen

An unscheduled entr'acte in the Savoy opera has delayed the climactic moment when the directors pick a chairman – patricians v. plebeians, like the great council-chamber scene in *Simon Boccanegra*. I had been looking forward to the choice of John Kemp-Welch, senior partner of Cazenove, the brokers whose five-star room service has cosseted the Savoy for so long. A Savoy chairman must be able to say: *Le patron mange ici.* That would present no problem, for as another Caz partner, Geoffrey Akroyd, put it: 'The Savoy is a jolly nice little place for lunch, and nice and handy, because you can get to it on a number 11 bus.' (13 November 1993)

Cut-price Ritz

For a big-hitting bonus earner – say, a general partner in Goldman Sachs – this Christmas offers the chance to buy an unusual present: the Ritz Hotel. Its owner, Trafalgar House, has reduced it to clear – from £85 million, the price marked in the books, to £20 million. This must leave it within the range of a capable Eurobond saleswoman. Better still, it opens the Ritz's revolving door to my plan for a customer buy-out, which would let all the Ritz's friends put the hotel pro rata on their bills. I hope that the ownership can be well spread before some greedy luncher signs for the hotel and gets it through his expense account disguised as a first-growth claret. My plan could be adapted to the Savoy, which may need it, one of these days. Its future could be secured by a whip round in the Grill Room, or Dealmakers' Arms, led by Sir Michael Richardson, Savoy director and dealmaker in chief.

As for the Ritz, now that Trafalgar is a protectorate of the great Jardine Matheson empire, I pin my hopes on Jardine's chairman, Henry Keswick, once an heroic proprietor of *The Spectator*. I have noticed him enjoying the Ritz's breakfast, which I rate the best in London. Try the kedgeree, Henry. (18/25 December 1993)

Poisson d'Or Savoyard

Foss v Harbottle (1843) is a leading case in company law, relating to the rights of minority shareholders. Giles Shepard was managing director first of the Savoy and then of the Ritz.

I fear the worst for Foss and Harbottle, Giles Shepard's learned goldfish, now that he is not at the Savoy to protect them. A friend claims to have seen them in the Grill on Wednesday, served *en colère*.

Only the other day I was consulting them on the law of trust. Suppose (I asked Foss) that a company – as it might be, an hotel group – had two classes of share, one with 20 times as many votes as the other. And suppose that some trusts owned enough of the high-voting shares to give them the keys to the company. These shares would command a premium? Quite so, said Foss. Then suppose (I went on) that another group of shareholders approached the trusts, offering them the prospect of a higher dividend if they would cede control. What would be the trustees' duty? No doubt at all, said Foss – it would be to secure for the trusts and their beneficiaries the greatest possible total return. If the trusts ceded control and handed the keys over, what would happen to the premium? It would vanish, said Foss. And what would that do to the total return? Put a minus sign in front of it, said Foss. And where would that leave the trustees? In the cart, said Foss. So what ought they to do? Break off the negotiations and take some more legal advice, said Foss – this one isn't over, it will run and run and I expect it to outlast my time, what do you think, Harbottle? Harbottle, through a mouthful of ants' eggs, concurred. (17 September 1994)

Put the Savoy on the bill

Angelo! I say, Angelo! Would you just put the hotel on the bill? In the Savoy Grill, sometimes known as the Dealmakers' Arms, the lunchers can see that their moment has come. That great trophy of their game, the Savoy stake, is up for sale once more. Passed from hand to hand for decades, it represents 69 per cent of the shares and in any other company would be a controlling interest. The Savoy game, though, is played by its own rules and these shares only carry 42 per cent of the votes – which has never been quite enough to prise loose the grip of the key shareholders so carefully installed by Sir Hugh Wontner. Over 40 years he saw off all the master financiers of the day, one after another. No one could have tried harder to outwit him than the Forte dynasty, or longer, but they have had to admit defeat.

Indeed, their own grip at Forte may now be prised loose. Granada's bid for Forte – great news for the dealmakers, encouraging them to new extravagances among the list of clarets – came with a pledge to sell off the Savoy stake. It would be denounced as a fruitless investment with a derisory yield, a symbol of obsession in the ruling family of what was no longer a family company. That looked a damaging and promising line of attack. Now Forte has felt obliged to match Granada's pledge, offering to sell the Savoy stake or to distribute it among its own shareholders. Granada might say (does say) that this rather makes its point. (9 December 1995)

Shepard's watch by night

Lupin could claim to have brought Nigel Lawson down; see p. 76.

see p. 76.

L*e Patron dort ici.* Giles Shepard, the new managing director of the Ritz, is working his way around the bedrooms, sleeping for himself. So the whirligig of time brings in his revenges. Before the Fortes forced him out a year ago, he had been managing director of the Savoy for 15 years. Now the battle has moved on, Forte is on the defensive, the dynasty has abandoned its long-held ambition and the Forte stake in the Savoy is up for sale.

As polished and elegant as his own tiepin, Mr Shepard is too civilised to gloat. He has been brought into the Ritz by its new owners, the Barclay brothers, who bought it for £75 million and have money left to spend on it. No sudden changes. I am encouraged to hope for the resurrection of the Rivoli Bar, where my late spaniel, Lupin, had visitor's rights and ate quite a lot of smoked salmon. As for the Savoy, Mr Shepard likes my idea of a customer buy-out – we agree that lunchers should qualify for share-meals, on the lines of air-miles. Not at the Ritz, though. (16/23 December 1995)

With love from the Savoy

Let the Savoy Hotel be first to wish us all a happy Christmas. It can look back on a year in which it finally outlived its most persistent suitor, the Forte group, but it was stuck with funeral expenses of £600,000 and is now splashing out on a restorative facelift. So to help cover its costs it has come up with a nifty line in Christmas gifts. For £4 you can buy a pound of Savoy coffee (£5 if you want the presentation tin) and, for rather more, a Savoy bed. This comes handmade and bespoke from the craftsmen of the Savoy Bedworks. Think of paying anything from £1415 to more than twice that. I suppose that, after a really gratifying stay at the Savoy, you might want to put the bed on the bill – an apter souvenir than a bathrobe or a tin of coffee. (21 September 1996)

Place of honour

The Hyde Park had a special place among Forte's grand hotels – revaluing its wine cellar helped to justify a Forte profit forecast – but now that Granada is breaking the collection up, it is the first to go. I hope that its new owners, the Mandarin Oriental group, will find a way to honour one of the Hyde Park's most stalwart customers, Evelyn Waugh. This was where he stayed, reporting on the audibility of farts through bedroom doors, and where he ordered dinner for 18 on the occasion of his daughter's coming-out, specifying: 'Non-vintage champagne for everybody except me.' (23 November 1996)

I'm on the bandwagon

My host at the Savoy Grill (or Dealmakers' Arms) rather pointedly ordered a bottle of mineral water. 'Do you find it difficult,' he asked, 'to drink at lunchtime, these days?' I reassured him: 'It gives me no trouble at all – yes, thank you, the usual, Angelo – it's working in the afternoon that I find harder.' All this is now to be regulated by the government's National Alcohol

Plan. Employers will be required to make rules for their staff, telling them what they can drink and when, on or off duty. This is something else for managements to do, apart from the residual chore of trying to run their businesses, and I shall be happy to offer them the City and Suburban Code.

Some excerpts follow: Champagne: never too early for. Meetings, board, annual general: will accelerate naturally to a close as one o'clock approaches. Sound effects (glasses and ice) help. Naps, post-prandial: an essential health requirement. Sofas should be provided. Port: incompatible with operating heavy machinery, such as word-processors or telephones. Whisky: one or more pub doubles advised before attending Treasury parties. Wine: red or white? An inappropriate choice, frequently offered by publicists. Even more depressing with cheese. It occurs to me that this plan will need a regulator, called Offwagon, and a National Alcohol Authority. Bags I be chairman of the hospitality committee. (12 August 2000)

Angelo maestoso

The campaign to save the Savoy Grill for the nation, or at least for the City, is gaining momentum. Angelo Moresca, the Grill's revered maître d', was Carol Leonard's guest of honour at the Christmas party thrown by Leonard Hull, her firm of head-hunters. Dealmakers from Sir Michael Richardson sideways, horrified by the Savoy management's idea that their canteen should be closed down and gussied up, rallied round with offers of support, moral and financial. All that they ask of him is promotion, from a table in the middle of the room to one of the banquettes. (7 December 2002)

Plaice on the bill

One wartime evening, Sir Olaf Hambro, chairman of the family bank, looked in at Wiltons for his solitary dinner and was told that, what with the Luftwaffe and the fish queues, the 200-year-old restaurant would have to close. He ate in silence, and then said, 'Put this place on the bill.' Still in family ownership, Wiltons has outlasted Hambros Bank itself, as a kind of cheerful club of well-heeled fish-fanciers with Sir Olaf's eldest grandson, Rupert Hambro, as chairman. (Tip: the nursery food is the best, so order the plaice and your credit card will come back in one piece.) Now comes a dynastic shift, with Rupert handing over to his brother Rick and keeping the next generation of Hambros in reserve. (19 April 2003)

Bankers, banquettes

One-upmanship sweeps the City: 'I'm going to the Savoy Grill's relaunch party.' 'Oh, are you? I was asked to one of the preview lunches. Doll's-house helpings.' The Dealmakers' Arms reopens this week after an anxious few months. The new chef attacked the tastes of his conservative customers, and they have had to be mollified by Angelo Maresca, the masterly maître d'hôtel. They will recover from the reupholstering of their banquettes, but I wonder whether the markets, in their subdued state, have enough dealmakers to go round. Some investment bankers have lost their jobs, others have lost their bonuses and with them as much as 90 per cent of their incomes, Now they may be changing their habits. In the City, I notice empty tables in the restaurants *[a cyclical phenomenon]* but crowded scenes in the Corney & Barrow wine bars. Thirst things first. (10 May 2003)

Sauce Savoyarde

Fishknives at dawn at the Dealmakers' Arms. The clash of wills at the Savoy Hotel between the Grill's modish new chef and his unreconstructed City customers is turning ugly. Only the other day an habitual luncher, perched on his accustomed banquette, waved the menu away and asked for some plainly grilled turbot. 'Yes, sir.' And a little hollandaise sauce? 'I will inquire, sir' – but the waiter returned, looking blank: 'The chef is not making *sauce hollandaise* today, sir.'

This scene was foreshadowed a century ago by Arnold Bennett in *The Grand Babylon Hotel*, his novel set, in all but name, in the Savoy: 'Situated on the Embankment, first in expensiveness, first in exclusiveness, first in that mysterious quality known as style.' In the Grand Babylon, Theodore Racksole, under pressure from his daughter, dares to order fillet steak for two and a bottle of Bass. His request is referred to Mr Rocco, the chef, who turns it down: 'He regrets to be unable to serve steak and Bass tonight, sir.' At this Mr Racksole leaves the room, buys the hotel, and gets the dinner he wanted.

Today's dealmakers may care to test whether Blackstone, the investment group which now owns the Savoy, would be open to offers *[yes, it was]*. The hollandaise could be thrown in. (5 July 2003)

The City is out to lunch and going west

The City is drifting westwards, and Angelo Maresca is showing the way. For two decades he was the impresario of the Savoy Grill. Then the management ordered a revamp, and Mr Maresca retired gracefully – but now that he is popping up again, with equal grace, to help Sir Rocco Forte give the kiss of life to Brown's Hotel, will the dealmakers go with him? They would have to hack their way across to the West End of London, but some of them are there already.

Lazards, a great City name, has moved out of its nondescript City office and set up shop in suitable style, round the corner from Mr Maresca. The Fleming family sold its bank in the City and has started again in the Bishop of Ely's eighteenth-century townhouse in Dover Street, well placed for the Ritz and the Caviar House. The Hambros moved west long ago, and Rupert is based in the floors above Wiltons, the family's restaurant. One motive, even stronger than lunch, drives the dealmakers. They need to be close to the customers.

Times have changed, and although the City stands where it did, the shocking truth is that some of its putative customers now find it a bus ride too far. Private bankers look after their flocks from behind discreet brass plates in Mayfair and St James's. Clients like theirs may have flown from the Gulf (or even Moscow) and think that they have done enough to reach the part of London where the hotels and shops and restaurants and clubs are – why go further? Tycoons, too, may measure their day's work in terms of distance from the airport. Corporate head offices have been moving in that direction. BP has abandoned its Lutyens palazzo in the City for St James's Square. Imperial Chemical Industries wanted to be near the Heathrow Express, which, when on form, takes 15 minutes from Paddington Station. Kingfisher and Marks & Spencer have opted for Paddington Basin.

A City friend saw this coming when he was urged to move his investment bank to Docklands. 'It's hard enough,' he told me, gesturing down the river, 'to get clients to come this far...' Now the City finds itself caught between two fires – between the lures of the West End and the pull of the financial factories on its eastern horizon, clustered round Canary Wharf. Their competitive advantages are real but could not be said to include location. An earlier generation of bankers lost heavily by lending to Canary Wharf, a new generation is thinking of buying it out, something like £2 billion of public money has been spent on roads and railways to support it, but it still takes 25 stops on the Tube, and one change of line, to get from Canary Wharf to Heathrow.

No wonder the investment banks have bought their own town-houses, far from their factories, where they can meet their clients. Dealmakers who still have the choice are likely to go where the business is, and I expect that more of the City's business will go west. (23 August 2003)

Spot the synergy

I have not thought it right until now to comment on the affairs of Hollinger International, parent company of *The Spectator* – but I see synergy in the approach from the Barclay brothers. They already own the Ritz. I look forward to a euphoric future of joint promotions and staff discounts. There will be special room rates for readers who, wanting to capitalise on their houses, elect to sell up and move in. (24 January 2004)

"My City host at Corney & Barrow insisted on ordering the Julienas. 'Look how the wine list describes it,' he said, 'just like me: rich, powerful and aromatic.'"

PART III

HONG
KONG
WEST

CHAPTER ELEVEN

OLD CITY, NEW CITY

Reconstructing an offshore financial centre on the north shore of the Thames

I once sailed to the Canary Islands from Canary Wharf. The Fred Olsen Line's ships used to chug out of the docks and down the river and come back from Tenerife, laden with tomatoes. Now the dockside warehouses have given way to gleaming towers, and the new City's satellite town sometimes threatens to overshadow its parent. If Canary Wharf is the most obtrusive sign of expansion and change, there are others, some of them subtler, as they should be. I have always argued that the City is a collection of markets, and thrives, as markets do, on variety, and that its built environment needs to reflect this. Financial factories are apt to yield production-line results.

Where there's brass

Rash iconoclasm sweeps the City. From the Government broker to the senior bill-workers, no monument can be counted secure. Worst of all, vandalous pick hammers have fallen on Gunton's Grotto – the City's noblest, most spacious, most convenient convenience. All roads led to it – Lombard, Threadneedle, Poultry, Cornhill. Its splendours of brass and marble and mahogany were inaugurated in 1881, as a polished plaque recorded, by Alderman Josiah Gunton. What a ceremony that must have been! What an assemblage of furred gowns, and silk hats, and chains! Now it stands desolate, like a partially excavated tomb – a wooded palisade surrounding a dismal cavity, a heffalump trap for the equestrian statue of the Duke of Wellington.

Who foresaw, or rather failed to foresee, what would happen when the City became, as it has, the stage for demonstrations? The protestors assemble in great numbers, bringing a day's supply in tins and bottles. Then they find themselves repulsed at the palisades and, turning in their tracks, ascend the broad steps of the Royal Exchange. There the lately installed market in financial futures has found itself overwhelmed by unauthorised and irregular transactions on the spot. Turn again, Aldermen! Commission a structure equal to the site and the need (preferably not by Mies van de Rohe) and aspire to hear posterity bless your names along with Gunton's! I offer, on being suitably primed with champagne at the Greenhouse bar around the corner, to re-inaugurate the place myself. (16 June 1984)

New built

Peter Palumbo's tower block – Mansion House Square to its friends, the City Stump to its enemies – soars towards heaven. On one side skulk the forces of reaction: decadent, affected conservationists, willing to see no good in the new and imaginary virtues in the old, imposing their caprice of taste as a dead hand upon change. On the other, observe the dynamic City, supplier of financial services to the world, bursting out of the constraints of Victorian buildings, eager for the new. In its present buildings the City manages to earn a net £5,400 million for the balance of payments, and is always pleased, and often surprised, to be appreciated. It is for others to debate the merits of Mies van der Rohe's design and Peter Palumbo's plan, as architecture and as townscape. What City and Suburban can properly consider is the charge that the plan's opponents are holding back the working City.

It is clearly not a charge which impressed the City Fathers. It has received no public support from any representative body in the working City. The weight both of argument and of sentiment is the other way. The City thrives on variety and individuality: the plan represents regimentation. In the alleyways, up the staircases of the old buildings, in modest offices seeing out the ends of their leases, new businesses can quickly seed. One of the City's most remarkable businesses, a world leader in modern communications, started in that way, only 20 years ago, in an attic (and before that, according to some histories, in a telephone box). The same friendly conditions have helped to grow that mixture of shops and meeting places, pubs and clubs, which are in their way an advantage for the City over the anonymity of other financial centres.

Just as there is more to a house than a *machine à habiter*, so there is more to an office, or a City of offices, than a *machine à travailler*, and a City designed for battery hens will produce quantity, which any fool can arrange, rather than quality, by which it must live. Lastly, it is not clear that even as a *machine à travailler*, this machine is the best model on the market. Much has changed since it was designed. Electronics have put their own stamp both on offices and on the businesses which use them. A leading City investment bank is thinking of moving a large part of its operations into a dockside warehouse, because there, and there alone, it can have one huge and tall dealing room. That bank and its fellows should not let their indifference to the Mansion House Square plan be misconstrued as support. (11 May 1985)

Threatened monument

The developers' pick looms over the Hambros' stately City home, which no listing protects. It houses the family merchant bank, which the Hambros with the votes want to sell. Hambros has a long lease on the building, but the landlords are already asking £50 million for the freehold. They are headed by P&O, which under Sir Jeffrey Sterling is a property company as well as a shipping line: Hambros has a useful stake in P&O. The bank, whoever may own it, will probably move out next year. That will leave a prime City site in Bishopsgate, occupied by what we shall surely told is an uneconomic building.

Behind its 1920s brick-and-stone façade in bankers' Queen Anne is the last of the classical merchant banks. The marble gleams, the dark wood glows. There is a high banking hall. There is a parlour, from the days when merchant bankers sat and worked together in parlours (not a bad way to work, either). There are dark club-like waiting rooms, where visitors can doze in leather chairs or break their fingernails picking at the leather bindings in the bookshelves (Hambros did not think it necessary to provide books). The building is not listed. The City planners themselves are sensitive just now to jibes that they protect and forbid too much, and so drive business away to new financial complexes in the docks or even at Victoria station. They should, all the same, remind themselves how Union Discount kept its fine late-Victorian banking hall and parlours, with plenty of room for the banking methods of the electronic age. (22 February 1986)

Sleeping partners

Coming shortly to the City: the Threadneedle Street Hotel. The planners have blessed it and the Merchant Taylors are behind it. (Their hall will be next door.) It must face competition, though, for the City is suddenly sprouting hotels – two under construction and five more with planning permission. Behind them in the queue is a riverside hotel off Lower Thames Street, designed by Terry Farrell and featuring a rooftop bar. Between them they will offer 1,370 new bedrooms, which will be a test of the City's initiative, but it does bear out my theory that the place has turned its back on finance and is being reborn as a theme park. No wonder Harvey Nichols wants to join in. If there must be a Threadneedle Street Hotel, though, the obvious candidate is further down the street. As Lutyens told Montagu Norman, the Bank of England would be just the place for a *thé dansant*. (27 June 1988)

Bombed out

The Baltic Exchange – home of the City's shipbroking market – had been irreparably damaged by an IRA bomb on 10 April.

I am sad at the destruction of the Baltic Exchange. An opulent mercantile cathedral built of purple marble, it seemed to reflect the Greek Orthodox taste of its ship-owning clients. Potato futures were celebrated in the south transept. The Baltic was a monument – and too few remain – of the Edwardian City. I could sooner have spared many more recent buildings, and their owners, given the state of the property market, could spare them too. (18 April 1992)

How time flies

Intrepid are the birdmen of London City Airport. The £135,000-a-yard tunnel under Limehouse basin, which took minutes off my journey from Billingsgate Market to Fishmongers Hall, seems to have gone to their heads. On tasteful posters, they have begun to advertise their dockside strip as being 20 minutes from the West End. From Piccadilly Circus, for instance: you take the Piccadilly Line (three stops) to Holborn, then the Central Line (seven stops) to Stratford, then the North London Line (every 20 minutes) to Silvertown and a brisk walk to the airport. Or to Embankment on the Bakerloo Line, for Charing Cross pier, hoping to catch the river bus on its 25-minute voyage to the Isle of Dogs – thence by a land bus which the birdmen lay on. Or you could blow the expense and take a taxi, which after 20 minutes on a normal weekday would be somewhere near the Monument with another six miles still ahead. Or you could wait for the Jubilee Line, though if you have not arrived by the end of the century the banks will want their money back. Or you could return to the Piccadilly Line and go to Heathrow. (29 May 1993)

Twenty-minute wonder

William Charnock, the intrepid birdman who runs London City Airport, has written to *The Spectator* in support of its claim to be 20 minutes from the West End. I doubt it, he doesn't: 'All our staff,' he says, 'are telling me...' The question is easily resolved. I invite Mr Charnock to join me in the West End for a mid-morning glass of champagne at the Ritz. We shall then go out and take a taxi to his airport. If we get there in 20 minutes or less I will pay £10 a minute to a charity of his choice – £10 for 20 minutes, £20 for 19 and so on. If we don't, he may like to pay £10 a minute to a charity of mine. Afterwards, I can make my own way back by public transport – brisk walk, North London Line, Central Line, Piccadilly Line. I like trains. (19 June 1993)

We have lift-off...

'The ring of steel': security measures introduced in response to the IRA bombing campaign.

Triumph for the intrepid birdman of London City Airport. William Charnock and I met at the Savoy on Monday morning, to test his claim that his airport could be reached from the West End in 20 minutes. It was the first day of the ring of steel (well, bollards, really) round the City, and I thought that this was guaranteed to jam the traffic for miles. Instead it frightened everyone off. At the Savoy's river entrance we found a taxi in suspicious readiness, and raced down empty roads, passing the Tower in six minutes and reaching the airport in 18. Hats off to Mr Charnock and his airport, which has many of the best qualities of Marylebone station. I have settled our bet, paying £20 (£10 per minute) to the Macmillan Cancer Relief Fund, but I missed my stipulated glass of champagne. The Savoy bar was shut, and the airport bar had been drunk dry the night before. (10 July 1993)

Occupational hazard

I was taken to St Bartholemew's Hospital when I fell down the stairs in the City Pram and Toy Shop. I had called in on my way back from lunch – in those days a stock-market lunch might conclude with iced kummel – to buy ping-pong balls for my cat. Barts in its capable way screened the damage, patched me up, sent me home and forbore to ask about the kummel.

I am saddened to think that this week, for the first time in centuries, the doors of Barts' accident and emergency wards have been shut – at the behest of some myopic don who can see that Barts is in the City and that nowadays not many people live there, No more they do, at midnight. It is at midday that they are most vulnerable – to stress in their offices, to injuries sustained in health clubs, to collisions with low-flying couriers, and even to the temptations of lunch and the hazards that might follow. Thanks to Barts I have so far survived them. (4 February 1995)

Wren's eye view

From the chimney-top of Bankside Power Station you can see St Paul's. This will be an added attraction when the chimney is turned into an observation tower, thanks to the £50 million of millenary funding that is to transform Sir Giles Gilbert Scott's handsome brick powerhouse into the Tate Gallery's presence on the south bank.

I hope that some of the money will buy back for Bankside the greatest townscape of them all – the view across the river that Wren saw from his site office on Cardinal's Wharf. This, as I found the other day, now commands a view of the office building occupied by the Swiss Bank Corporation, with bits of St Paul's peeping over the top. No other building in London, not even the Department of the Environment's own, could so much improve its environment by falling down. A cheque from the Millennium Commission could give it the push it needs. (4 November 1995)

Folies de grandeur

At 600 feet, the NatWest Tower will no longer be the tallest branch bank in the country. It was designed as a showpiece head office – always a bad sign in banks – but took so long to build that the top brass went off it and stayed where they were. I remember asking Alex Dibbs, their cheery chief executive, when it was going to be finished. He rocked with laughter: 'Hoo! Hoo! Well, Christopher, how old are you?' Driven out of it by the IRA's bomb, the National Westminster is not returning and will look for tenants. They will find the building handsome but impractical, a thin skin of offices draped around a core of 21 lift shafts. At that it knocks spots off Barclays' bulbous new head office in the Moorish taste, where the top nine floors are still, understandably, to let. (9 December 1995)

Room for a view

Two unrepeatable holes have opened up in the City of London. Enjoy them while they last. One, in St Martin's le Grand, marks the site of a nondescript office block, whose absence now unmasks the noble classical façade of Goldsmith's Hall, Philip Hardwick's masterpiece. The other is where Slater Walker used to be. That loss will not be felt, and the gain is a perspective from Queen Victoria Street to the south front of St Paul's – last shown up to such advantage after the bombs had stopped falling. Too soon this spectacular hole will be plugged by a London home for Nissho Iwai, whatever that may be, and in front of Goldsmith's Hall will rise a speculative office block, possibly no more descript than its predecessor. I urge the Corporation of London to think again and adopt a policy of set-aside, which would leave these holes open for public enjoyment *[no such luck]*. (13 April 1996)

Up in the clouds

The 'Erotic Gherkin' was commissioned by Swiss Re to occupy the site of the old Baltic Exchange.

The tallest and vainest building in Europe emerged this week from Sir Norman Foster's drawing board, accompanied by puffs of pure fatuity. It will come in handy in the City, its promoters say, because banks are merging and will need bigger offices. Banks, like most businesses, want smaller offices and fewer of them. That is one reason why they are merging. This tower would look down on NatWest's tower, which is empty, on Barclays' bulge, which is also empty, and on Sir Brian Pitman at Lloyds Bank who has devoured Hill Samuel and TSB, shut their head offices, fired most of the inhabitants and fitted the rest into Lloyds' own stately home in Lombard Street.

Another puff says that this tower would serve the City as a virility symbol. Margaret Thatcher was urged to adopt a strong pound as a virility symbol. She declined, saying that she did not need one. The City, too, can keep its pecker up without Sir Norman's help. I rely on its Court of Common Council to throw stones at his glasshouse. The Court might reflect that this proposal comes to it from Trafalgar House, which owns Cunard (two black balls at the masthead: I am proceeding in circles out of control) and, until it fell into the arms of some Norwegians, could claim to be our least successful major public company of the decade. Its tower would replace the bombed Baltic Exchange. I would put it back. (14 September 1996)

The Square Theme Park

Prescott's Bank in Cornhill was an eighteenth-century City survival. The Prescotts were long gone (to Hull?) and their bank was a branch of the National Westminster, but it kept its decorous hall, its mahogany pillars and counters, its coffered ceiling, its handsome glass dome… It looked quite like a pub, in fact, and now it is one, thanks to Fullers the brewers, who have reopened it in fine style as the Counting House.

So the City moves on to its new life as a theme park. NatWest, with a plethora of marble halls, has turned one into a picture gallery and another can be hired for suitably grand parties, while its tower, with its new portico of steel and glass, will soon have a café and is now collecting tenants who like their rooms to have views. How long before the Old Broad Street branch, which has its own swimming pool, becomes a health club? *[It has already happened.]* Now the Prudential has nerved itself to move out of its massive Victorian pile. Across Holborn the Pearl's palace stands empty and the Pru's estate agents will have to use their ingenuity. *C'est magnifique mais ce n'est pas la gare.* Perhaps it could be the City's only country-house hotel. *[The former Pearl Assurance building did indeed become a luxury hotel, the Renaissance London Chancery Court.]*(14 February 1998)

Down, down, down

The Millennium Hole in the City of London – site of that hideous block on the corner of Fenchurch Street, before Barclays pulled it down – has set a good example. The oppressive concrete bastion across the moat from the Tower of London is doomed. The big insurance brokers Marsh & McLennan inherited it when they took over Bowrings, but now they think that a hole in the ground would be prettier. How right they are about that. Timed for the millennium, a stylish Norman Foster building is to replace it. Now let us see the Stock Exchange follow suit. Its drab tower has long ceased to serve the purpose for which was built. In white tie, tails and metal, I was there to see the Queen open it. I hope to be there when she shuts it, but if she is too busy, I am prepared to stand in. What a hole it will make. (23 May 1998)

Fish and chips

The worst news from the City all year comes from Leadenhall Market, where I find the shutters down at Ashdowns. The market itself, with its red and gold Victorian iron-work and high glass roof, puts its ostentatious neighbour, Lloyd's of London, in its place. Ashdowns is or was its superlative fish shop, with the jaunty Captain 'Beechey' Blackett presiding in straw hat and Wellington boots and (for the occasion) the sandwich board that he wore to picket Lloyd's. His smoked salmon was once deemed too expensive for the Bank of England but I saw no need to make such economies. Alas, Ashdowns has had troubles with its own financing, and these now threaten to overwhelm it. Surely its resourceful City customers can find a remedy? If not, it will be time to pull the shutters down on the City. (28 November 1998)

Cornhill's their oyster

A warm — well, *chambré* — welcome to Lay & Wheeler, the Colchester wine merchants. They have moved into a handsome Victorian bank (Lloyds was there last) in Cornhill, and will open a wine and seafood bar, matching their excellent Chablis to Colchester oysters. So the relaunch of the City of London as a theme park rumbles forward. Down the road from Cornhill, an ancestral banking hall in glass, mahogany and marble now houses a restaurant and brasserie, much to the surprise of the head of the dynasty. 'It must be a jolly good restaurant,' he says, 'to make more money than a bank.' (8 April 2000)

Towers don't flower

Just what the City doesn't need: another tower block. This one, at an insalubrious corner of Houndsditch, will be twice the height of St Paul's, and was nodded through this week by the City fathers. Towers, as they ought to know, have never bloomed in the City. Their own, on their estate in the Barbican, are relics of an outdated attempt to show off. Most of the space in NatWest's tower (now sold) was taken up by lift shafts. Lloyd's ordered a spoof high-tech building (sold again the other day) to accommodate a business that used pencils and paper. The Stock Exchange is moving into Paternoster Square and leaving its drab tower behind it. The Swiss Re's 600 ft Zeppelin standing on its nose is much admired, but may struggle to find tenants whose furniture fits into circular offices. The City has and will have plenty of space on the developers' hands without the Tower of Houndsditch. (17 January 2004)

Going cheep

Canary Wharf is up for sale again. Five years ago, when it was floated, I said that I would just as soon it sank. The project's charms have decreased since we learned that tower blocks in financial centres are vulnerable. I doubt whether the banks would have put so many of their eggs in such a basket now. They were lured there by tax breaks, still with us and reckoned to have totted up to £2 billion. On top of that goes the money spent in support of a commercial development which became a pet project of governments. It failed on all three tests of property – location, location and location – so it needed a toy railway, and the most expensive road (in pounds per inch) in Europe, and an upgrade of the toy and an extension of the Tube. Put all that in at £1 billion or more, and add, if you like, the money lost when, not so long ago, Canary Wharf went bust. Its banks took a haircut and its unsecured creditors were left with a mere 15p in the pound. There is still time to tow it out to sea and sink it. (27 March 2004)

Two-day wonder

To be the grandest hotel in the City is not saying much, so I wish the Great Eastern well. Sir Terence Conran has restored it and reopens it this week. This monument to the railway age had fallen on hard times. A City friend of mine, against his better judgement, once tried to book a visitor in. He asked the girl at the desk for a room for two days and her eyes widened. 'Most of the gentlemen,' she said, 'only book for two hours.' (26 February 2000)

CHAPTER TWELVE

GOODBYE TO ALL THAT

A cheerful farewell to the old City life (and welcome to Hong Kong West)

I have only once been prompted to write the City's obituary. This was when Barclays abandoned its attempt to build up an investment bank and put it through the shredder. As so often happened at Wimbledon, the last British hope was out of the tournament, though we could still provide the stadium and sell the strawberries. This, I said, marked the demise of the City, which would have to be relaunched as Hong Kong West. Britain, just like China, would have a financial entrepot in its bottom right-hand corner: one country, two systems. Thus far the model has prospered, but it still needs the old City's virtues. Keep your fingers crossed for it.

Off with his hat

A fearful omen from the money market is the fate of the Earl of Clarendon's hat. Tall black burnished silk hats are the market's uniform. Lord Clarendon (7th earl, cr. 1776) is the chairman of bill-brokers Secombe Marshall & Campion, and, in point of noble precedence within the market, second only to Gerrard & National's deputy chairman, the Earl of Eglinton and Winton (18th, cr. 1507). Setting off to call upon banks, and, of course, correctly turned out, he was walking through the City when, without warning, he found his hat snatched from his head. He stood in astonishment while the snatcher made good his escape. The hat is still missing. The market is at a loss. Some liken it to the theft of King Baudouin's ceremonial sword at the independence of the Belgian Congo, others, classically brought up, to the mutilation of the herms in ancient Athens. (24 May 1986)

Truncheons against punks

A demo in the sacred Square Mile – whatever next? Answer, no doubt another several. They have become quite familiar: miners marching through with bands and banners, or occasional Stop the City days, when the place is invaded by (mostly cheerful) anarchists, known to the beleaguered inhabitants as Punks Against Profits. Old heads shake glumly. When, they ask, was the City ever subject to such indignities? In the Gordon Riots? In the Peasants' Revolt – when the Lord Mayor knifed Wat Tyler and earned the City the dagger in the first quarter of its coat of arms? But perhaps peace in the City is a rarity. H. G. de Frayne, who joined the Bank of England almost 100 years ago, describes in his memoirs the scene he found:

> Unemployment was rife... Day after day men in their thousands poured along Cornhill and King William Street with banners saying 'Give us Work or Bread!' and here and there

'We will have Work or Bread!' They looked half-starved and hopeless to me, with very little fight in them. But there were of course professional trouble-makers amongst them, and there was widespread damage and looting in the West-End. The Old Lady, after consultation with the City Police, sounded the alarm and called for volunteers from the staff as special constables.

De Frayne was issued with a pair of armlets and a large wooded truncheon, which had apparently been kept in reserve since the Chartist riots of 1848. It would, he said, have broken any head that hit it. Today's City men, and maybe today's punks, do not know what they are missing. (4 November 1984)

Now, boys, light the blue touch-paper and stand close

27 October was the day of 'Big Bang', when the London Stock Exchange switched to 'dual capacity' trading, allowing brokers and jobbers (or market-makers) operating within the same firms.

My friend the stockjobber closed his book, turned his back on his pitch, and walked with me off the Stock Exchange floor, down Throgmorton Street and into Bill Bentley's fish house. We raised our glasses of Montrachet to the last of the good old days. On Monday he must quit the floor and settle down at his workstation, one of hundreds (seniority and guile secured him the station nearest the exit and the loo) in a huge carpeted financial factory arranged, like all smart City factories, round an atrium. A deputy will man his pitch, empowered to deal on a modest scale, but not, like my friend, to make or lose on his own book a million pounds in a day. The big deals will come upstairs, to be made over the telephone and the screen, from atrium to atrium. Already, he says, the floor (though it seems its usual bustling self to me) is a place of the past: 'There's no atmosphere here any more.'

The talk is all of the weekend's dress rehearsal ('If we're going to deal wearing suits, we may as well practise wearing suits') for Big Bang Day. A bad dress rehearsal, I say helpfully, means a good first night. He suspends judgement. There were brokers, he says, trying to carry the weekend's Monopoly-money dealings forward into real money. Some came to blows, and one found the rebuke: 'After all, it's only a game!' Practising on their screens, one dealer offered a price and another sold. The price dropped by twopence, he sold again, another twopence off, another sale… 'How long are we going on like this?' 'As long as you like, old boy – you've got the big figure wrong, your price is a pound too high.' When the high-stake games of Space Invaders begin on Monday, that sort of mistake could cost an atrium. (25 October 1986)

Shares for none

It is a sad sign of such times that a respected City editor has told his staff that he proposed to forbid them to own any shares directly, and to extend the ban to their wives and children. He could and should have reminded them that they, too, hold their information on behalf of their employer – and with all that follows from that. But next, I suppose, in view of the state of the roads and to avoid any accidents which may lead to misunderstandings, the motoring correspondent will be made to travel by train. (13 December 1986)

Roughing it

The City, I must say, has always been fond of its flowers. A Victorian occasion saw the City Horticultural Society addressed by the Rothschild of the day. Clerks in their thousands, eager to hear the secrets of the great Rothschild plantations and hothouses at Exbury and Tring, had delayed their returns to their own trim and modest patches. The speaker beamed benevolently and began with a word of advice. 'No garden,' he told them, 'how-

ever small, should be without an acre or two of rough woodland.'
(10 September 1988)

Purple sprouting bank

Barclays Bank has set up its Lombard Street head office with supersmart word-processors which know how to spell. Dash away at the keyboard and the machine tidies up for you, automatically taking any surplus 'r' out of 'harass' and putting it safely into 'embarrass'. The word processors have a 42,000-word vocabulary, but it does not include the word 'Barclays'. The programmers forgot it. Consequently, anyone typing 'Barclays' on the Barclays system finds it automatically corrected to the nearest word in the vocabulary. This has proved to be 'broccoli'. Dear Sir, on behalf of – oh, blast, there it goes again... City companies have their nursery nicknames (the Notional Wetmonster, the Comical Onion) and I welcome the Banco di Broccoli. (22 October 1988)

Winning over Morgan

Across the road from the Bank of England sits the statue of George Peabody, honoured as philanthropist and merchant banker – a singular combination – and the founder of Morgan Grenfell. I am keeping an eye on old George. If he splits, cracks or develops a tendency to whirl round and round in his marble chair, I shall know what he thinks at seeing his proud house become an outstation of the Deutsche Bank. There were bigger merchant banks when I came to the City, and even better ones – my City Editor on *The Times*, Ansell Egerton, kept a headline in standing type: FIRST WIN FOR MORGAN – but none was better connected.

It can be argued that Morgan's trouble began when they started to win. Let us say, without reopening old wounds, that they pressed too hard and nearly brought the house down. We can also say that when with the Bank of England's blessing John Craven arrived as chief executive, a deal could not be far behind. Mr Craven is one of the great international dealmakers of the day. Indeed, to gain his services Morgan had to buy his company, and Mr Craven received £5 million of Morgan's convertible loan stock, which must now be well worth converting. In the approach to Big Bang, the Bank of England voiced its hope that the City would come out with half a dozen teams able to play the new game of international investment banking and to hold their places in the first division. Morgan certainly aspired to be among them, and would have been on most people's lists. Now, if you count the teams, you say: Warburg, Barclays Zoete Wedd. Then you cross your fingers and say: Kleinwort Benson. Then you cross them again and say: Um. (2 December 1989)

Tickled Pink

I am tickled pink to see the *Financial Times* in court, trying to stop the *Evening Standard* printing its City pages 'on FT Peach or any other shade of pink'. There were pink papers before the FT – sporting prints, in every sense; Bristol as late as the 1950s ran to two rival evening papers, in two shades: the Pink 'Un and the Green 'Un. (Which ecologically minded editor will pick that idea up?) My plans for an enhanced City and Suburban column include printing on a distinctive shade of champagne, possibly Veuve Clicquot. FT, keep off. (22 September 1990)

Toeing the line

Paparazzi photographs had appeared in the tabloid press of the Duchess and her so-called adviser canoodling beside a Riviera swimming pool.

I find City opinion divided on John Bryan. Some argue that the Duchess of York's financial adviser has exceeded the bounds of self-regulation. Others more robustly maintain that he can have done no more than financial advisers usually do to their clients. (29 August 1991)

Dear Mary, please copy

Note on City etiquette: a friend of mine was commissioning invitation cards from a printer who is also a friend. Engraving? Yes, certainly. Gilded edges, rounded corners? The printer shook his head. 'If you don't mind my saying so,' he explained, 'gilded edges and rounded corners are for Japanese bankers.' (7 March 1992)

More than human

A friend of mine has just been fired by her company's Director of Human Resources. This unctuous euphemism has crept into business life by a process that would have been familiar to Parkinson the Lawgiver, now departed. Just as a Director of Corporate Affairs is a public relations man with another PR man to do the work for him, and a PR agency on an expensive contract, a human resources supremo is a jumped-up personnel officer whose personnel policy is to employ more. They in turn will need their personal personnel assistants in numbers that will place new demands on the department, which must expand to meet them.

Companies thus develop elephantiasis of the hindquarters which causes their teeth to fall out. They find it harder to afford to pay people at the sharp end. That is where the axe falls, for a personnel department (still more, a human resources empire) has never been known to declare itself redundant. That has to be done for it. One of the High Street banks – where the idea has certainly been canvassed – would be a good place to start. Until then, it will be worth remembering that Director of Human Resources is a title properly belonging to Almighty God. (27 March 1993)

The Lord Mayor has trumpets and musketeers and pikemen, but no handle

Rolling through the City in his golden coach, Paul Newall succeeds this weekend as the 666th Lord Mayor of London, which puts him on the same number as the Beast in Revelations and in one respect is unlucky. The Blues and Royals, trumpets blowing, will escort him. Doggett's Coat and Badge Men will march before him, his sword bearer will attend him, his personal bodyguard of pikemen and musketeers will follow him, but he will have to get along as best he can without a handle. A baronetcy used to come with the job and, when that honour came to be reserved for the consorts of retiring prime ministers, Lord Mayors were made Knights Grand Cross of the Order of the British Empire.

I urge a more robust attitude. The City has always maintained its independence of ministers and sometimes of monarchs – Clarendon, the Stuarts' minister, called it the sink of all ill-humour in the kingdom – and it need not wait on them for honours. There were Lord Mayors of London before there were baronets (a Stuart revenue raiser) and long before there was a British empire, and they have watched enough heads roll on Tower Green to know that ministers are transient. (13 November 1993)

Second time unlucky for the lordly Barings – a great Nemesis overtakes Croesus

Barings had been ruined by the fraudulent dealings of Nick Leeson, a trader in its Singapore office, and was subsequently acquired for £1 by the Dutch group ING.

This, I thought, must be a time slip. 'Barings crashes – speculation blames': had I taken a wrong turning in the space–time continuum and come out in 1890? Or had some subeditor returning from a heavy lunch reached for the '105 years ago' column and put it on the front page?

The story of the Barings crisis is a City classic. The lordly family bank wakes up to find that its sanguine view of foreign markets could mean ruin. Rumours run through the City as senior bankers come in on a Saturday – a Hambro observed with a Rothschild in St Swithin's Lane at 8 o'clock in the morning... The Governor of the Bank of England asks the Chancellor for help, is turned down, and instead brings Barings' rivals to its rescue and, so they believe, their own. A Baring uncle rallies round, turning up with all his money in bulging Gladstone bags, one of which bursts while he is arguing with his cab driver about an overcharge of sixpence. A great Nemesis, he says, has overtaken Croesus. The family has to retrench, selling its pictures and sacking its under-butlers, but the Barings and their bank survives. The only scar to be seen a century later is the telltale comma in 'Baring Brothers and Co., Limited'.

Well, I thought, if this is the story I know how it ends. I was wrong about that. This time there was to be no saving Barings. The creditors' men are in, to put it up or break it up for sale. Byron in Don Juan yoked the Barings together with their hereditary rivals:

Who hold the balance of the world? Who reign
O'er congress, whether royalist or liberal?...
The shade of Buonaparte's noble daring?
Jew Rothschild, and his fellow-Christian Baring.

To the Barings, the Rothschilds were parvenus. When Nathan Mayer Rothschild was still on his way to Manchester (London came later) Sir Francis Baring was being accused of putting his own park fence round Hampshire. The plethora of peerages followed, matched only by the Cecils and Howards. Lord Derby, Queen Victoria's prime minister, offered Thomas Baring the Exchequer, but he thought the bank counted for more: 'Half my pleasure is to work for a house which we intend to be perpetual.' (4 March 1995)

Paying for the port

I wonder whether the fees for dismantling Lord Hanson's empire will be more than the fees for putting it together. Already the City stands to collect the thick end of £250 million in payments of one kind and another, to allow Granada to buy Forte and dismantle that. I forecast a change in the dealmakers' jargon: synergy will now give way to dysergy. The City professionals must watch the business scene as the dons of Scone College (in Evelyn Waugh's *Decline and Fall*) watched the revels of the Bollinger Club. They look forward to the fees as the dons looked forward to the fines, expecting to be kept in vintage port: 'It'll be more if they attack the chapel. Oh, please, God, make them attack the chapel.' (3 February 1996)

Off centre

The sadly prescient warning below referred to the terrorist bomb which went off in the basement of the World Trade Center in 1993.

I never cared for South Quay when I worked there. It was a charmless and pretentious building, miles away from anywhere that I might need or want to be. All the same, for the IRA to blow it up was a bit much. This unpleasantness seems to have been meant to harm London as a financial centre, although, as I say, no one could call the West India Dock central. The theory is that business will now go elsewhere. I do not foresee it. The sad truth is that all financial centres have their inconveniences and hazards. In Paris and Tokyo, stay clear of the metro. In New York, do not stand too close to the World Trade Center. As for Frankfurt, the nightlife there is limited and not available on Tuesdays, when she goes to Wiesbaden to see her auntie. (17 February 1996)

For love or money

I t pays to be nice to your bank manager. Such must have been the experience of the Turkish company which has just secured an $80 million facility from the International Finance Corporation, the enterprising end of the World Bank. The company's name is Arcelik. Now that is what I call relationship banking. (27 July 1996)

Mark of respect

Two minutes' silence is rare in the City, but on Monday 11 November at the eleventh hour it was observed. On the trading floor of Liffe, the financial futures exchange, the noisy, bouncy, bright-jacketed traders stood still. Only one sound could be heard, I am told – a whisper directed to some inattentive figure: 'Show some respect, you merchant banker.' This must be a term of abuse. (16 November 1996)

State of the Union

The Union Discount Company of London cannot be long for this world, and I shall miss it. For more than a century it was the money market's right marker. Arthur Trinder, its mightiest manager, would start his day at 11 with a gin and tonic and a smoked salmon sandwich. Later he might jam his top hat on his head and stroll across to the Bank of England to borrow, stubbing out his cigar on its pillars. When I first came to the City I would be sent into the Union's Victorian parlours, to ask how money was today. I was received there with kindness and patience. Union and the other discount houses lived by borrowing the spare money in the system and investing it to earn a profit. They bought (or discounted) the bills on London which, when Union was founded, had financed the trade of the world. They were part of a City based on privilege and obligation, which both came with their access to the Bank.

All that has gone. Now the Union has withdrawn from the money market, after heavy losses, and all that remains is to sell the company and to break it up. Foreseeing the day, I had plans for the Union's entrance hall, with its richly coloured tiles, mahogany counter, sweeping staircase and enticing balcony above. I wanted to reopen it as the Last Chance Saloon or as a house of ill fame. It deserved better. (1 March 1997)

Wimbledonised

Alexanders Discount had been founded in 1809, six years before Waterloo. Waterloo is the hinge of the action in *Vanity Fair* and Thackeray, writing 30 years later, is at pains to get his details right. So when old Mr Sedley is down on his luck and trying to talk his credit up, he drops the names of Rothschild and of Baring Brothers, and asserts: 'Alexander would cash my bill, down, sir, down on the counter, sir.' I knew it as a cornerstone of the money market, established in Lombard Street under the sign of the Artichoke, and run by the precise Charles Clinton Dawkins: 'That article was intimately, rather than well, informed.' Now a plain little pronouncement from the Bank of England lets us know that Alexanders has surrendered its banking licence and Sedley's counter has closed. Instead, the Bank has given a licence to the Housing & Commercial Bank, Korea.

So the Wimbledonisation of the City – we sell the strawberries, they field the players – wins another set. This week Mercury, the biggest and most successful of the City's independent fund managers, has sold itself out to an American buyer, for a fortune. I assume that Housing & Commercial is in better shape than the average Korean bank, but I cannot think that the next Thackeray will bother to include it. (22 November 1997)

There goes the vintage of 1762

For the City of London, 1762 was a vintage year. Francis Baring set up shop, and some numerate citizens set up the world's first mutual life assurance office. Some non-vintage years have followed, Barings had to be sold for a pound, and now its twin, the Equitable Life, is being hawked around the City, with its directors hoping for a suitably better price. Theirs is a wretched story. They tried to save their society's skin at the price of its reputation and have failed.

The facts are by now well established. The Equitable threw in guarantees when selling life assurance, made no investments to match them, and when they proved to be expensive tried to wriggle round them. Holders of policies with guarantees were told that their terminal bonuses would be scaled down so that the guarantees were not worth having.

Macbeth, as I observed, had the same trouble with the witches: 'Who keep the word of promise to our ears But break it to our hopes.' This was a hideous precedent. The Equitable had never needed to rely on witchcraft. Its record spoke for itself and its promises were well worth having. To call their worth into question would suggest that it could ill afford to meet them. That could only be damaging to the society and so to the interests of all its members, whether they held guarantees or not. Still the directors maintained that this was the right thing to do and that the law allowed them to do it. They were wrong about that. The result is a knock-out. After 238 years of happy mutuality, the Equitable is for sale. (29 July 2000)

There's life in the old City townhouse yet as Cazenove makes the weather

On a fine day the City feels like Hong Kong West: a global financial centre offshore of the Thames where nationality no longer matters. On a bad day I mourn the old City, which has given up its pretensions of leadership and is content to provide the centre court, but not the champions.

Cazenove is the exception and makes its own weather. Nothing could be more redolent of the old City, or, for that matter, old England, than the townhouse in Tokenhouse Yard with the rickety lift, the mahogany panelling, and the courteous denizens whose shoes are always polished and have laces. At the time of Big Bang, Caz stood out when other brokers were selling out, believing that it had a future as an independent firm and – more old-fashioned still – a partnership. 'We will never go public,' so Luke Meinertzhagen had said when he was senior partner. *(The firm had just announced a reversal of this policy.)* (2 December 2000)

Monsieur Numero

The Swiss banker was shocked. Round the City lunch table, after the port, came the visitors' book, and I saw his eyes widen. 'You mean to say,' he asked our host, 'that you expect your customers to sign their *names*?' (10 February 2001)

Must I get out of bed? Oh, yes, Sir Peter, just think of all your incentives

I am often surprised to see how much it takes to get business-men out of bed in the mornings. Sir Peter Bonfield, for one: without his daily cocktail of incentives he would just roll over. Most of us are motivated to work by the direct connection between earning and eating. Motivating the man in the top slot is more elaborate. He must have his basic salary (though not so basic as all that), but this is only the beginning. A golden handshake may allure him. He will expect a performance-linked bonus and may get another one, paid at discretion – sometimes for doing successfully what he was being paid to do in the first place. He must have his stock options and phantom shares, which can be just as good as real ones, and a long-term incentive plan, too. A decent period of notice will protect him from having all these good things snatched away, and his pension plan will keep him off the streets in his old age.

Consultants do well out of cooking up these schemes and swear that anything less will let the top man oversleep. Remuneration committees sit in judgement, which they tend to temper with mercy. They were merciful at Marks & Spencer to Luc Vandevelde, the executive chairman. He should still get his bonus, they thought, if only to cheer him on. In the end he was shamed out of it.

Sir Peter sees nothing to be ashamed about. He is the chief executive of British Telecom, where the board has had to pass the dividend and ask the shareholders to find £6 billion, but he still stands to collect £3 million this year, in salary, shares and a £481,000 bonus. (19 May 2001)

Buy cheaper, later

Depressed? Cheer yourself up with a glass of Château Pétrus. You can buy last year's vintage and get £2 change out of £10,000 a dozen. Your shares may be wilting but other assets seem to be immune – so far, that is. Clarets *en primeur* have been run up to unheard-of levels, even though Oddbins now has them in stock. Locomotive nameplates, too, fetch record prices, so my railway correspondent, I. K. Gricer, tells me. If you would rather have a Picasso, Phillips the auctioneers, who have a new rich owner, are selling modern pictures in New York next month, and have won the business by guaranteeing the proceeds. I would hope to buy cheaper, later. Stock markets, which live by anticipation, show the way to others, and their example may be followed by the costly assets, financed with borrowed money, which so many of us live in. (22 September 2001)

To know your customer, ask for her gas bill

We must hope that the Queen does not have her Jubilee spoiled by a letter from her bank, wanting to know who she is. She may be asked to show her gas bill. It is an open secret that her account is with Coutts, a suitably grand address where her family has banked since 1760, but grandeur and longevity are no defence against regulatory zeal and may even attract it. Established in 1672 and still family-owned, C. Hoare and Co. is senior to Coutts and in its way just as exclusive. Inquiries about opening accounts can be met with a counter-inquiry of 'Who's introduced you?' and prospective customers must be brought to the bank and presented.

Now Hoare's has been told to write to its customers asking for proof of identity. One of them, an old City hand, has banked there since 1960, but still got a letter from his manager: 'URGENT – ACTION REQUIRED. The banking industry's new regulators, the Financial Services Authority, are adopting a rigorous "Know your customer" policy. They require that the bank holds on file formal confirmation of the identity and address of all its customers. I would be grateful, therefore, if you could let the bank have certified copies of your passport pages showing the expiry date, your name and photograph, and a recent utility bill or other official correspondence showing your name and home address. These should be certified as true copies by a practising solicitor or accountant, bank manager or JP. A reply envelope is enclosed.'

On picking himself up, this customer found his manager full of apologies. The FSA's inspectors, the manager said, had come to Hoare's last December and soon told the bank that it did not know its customers. Where, they wanted to know, were the passport copies and the utility bills? It was put to the bank so forcefully, the manager said, that it more or less became a directive, and the bankers felt that they had to comply. Protests to the highest levels of the FSA have got them nowhere. If the FSA is working its way through the private banks, its next port of call must be Coutts, and some drafts of correspondence have already come into my hands:

Buckingham Palace
Dear Sirs, In reply to your letter, I am obliged to point out that Her Majesty does not have a gas bill. Gas is supplied to the Palace, but payment is adjusted by the Lord Chamberlain and the Keeper of the Privy Purse without her intervention. Nor, since a passport is a request for assistance issued by the Foreign Secretary in her name, is there any reason why she should direct one to herself. If you insist on pictorial identification, pull a tenner out of the till and have

a look. If a bank manager is good enough as a witness, why won't his word suffice? You must remember that, these days, you have competition. Lord Fellowes, who was until lately Her Majesty's Private Secretary, is now chairman of Barclays Private Bank and, should her account move his way, could certainly claim to know his customer. Now be good chaps and forget all this nonsense.

A. Cheesecutter-Hatt (Maj.), Sharp-Stick-in-Waiting

Coutts and Co, 440 Strand,
London WC2R 0QS
Dear Major Cheesecutter-Hatt, However much we might wish to forget about our regulators and their directives, we dare not. Their powers are draconian and their memories are elephantine. They have recently taken over responsibility for money laundering, or rather for preventing it, and they have to make sure that Osama bin Laden is not funding himself through our books. The effect of their rules is to make it harder for those without passports or gas bills to open accounts, though Her Majesty's ministers prefer to blame the banks for this, accusing us of financial exclusion. This would, unhappily but undoubtedly, be Her Majesty's own experience, were she to attempt to move her account somewhere else. Perhaps, in the circumstances, you could furnish us with a certified copy of the Prime Minister's recommendations for the Honours List? We could count this as official correspondence.

J. Nibb, Authorised Signatory

Buckingham Palace
Dear Nibb, You must be joking. You can take it from me that Mr bin Laden is not paying his bills through Her Majesty's private account. At one time or another she has guaranteed the overdrafts of a number of overextended

relations, but he is not one of them. Your letter suggests that her account could not be moved to another bank, since the FSA's rules apply to them all. I may tell you, in confidence, that we have been approached by the Banco Ticinese dei Conti Numerati, which is conveniently located by the lakeside in Lugano, Switzerland, is happy to offer Her Majesty every facility, and tells us that her money would be in excellent company! So pull your finger out, or kiss your Jubilee medal goodbye. Your MVO (fifth class), too.

A. Cheesecutter-Hatt (1 June 2002)

...and finally...

Must fly

L unching in Lombard Street, I was dismayed to find my fellow City scribes suddenly taking off like a flock of starlings. They would not wait for the coffee, let alone for the prospect of port and cigars. Now that their papers have abandoned their offices in Fleet Street and the City, they all had long journeys to make to distant destinations, east, west and south. It is as though they were missing their latchkeys, and were forced to look for them under the streetlamps of Poplar or Kensington, rather than in the place where they had been dropped and might be found. Not sharing their disadvantage, I accepted another glass of claret and sat tight. (24 March 2001)

EPILOGUE

Ever since the Lombards gave their name to a street of bankers, the City has flourished with its doors open to newcomers. Addison, in *The* (first) *Spectator*, conjured up the cosmopolitan traders at the Royal Exchange and called it an emporium for the whole earth. I hare been lucky to catch it at its most vital and inventive. For me, as for so many of its daily inhabitants, it has been a way of life.

It may be the model of the future. On or off the Thames's muddy shore is a marketplace which knows no frontiers, an example of globalisation in action, a financial emporium for the whole earth. For all that, it remains vulnerable – to taxmasters, to regulators, to tidy-minded Eurocrats who find its economic anarchy offensive, and to their political allies who envy London's advantage and would like to take it away.

Today's City draws on local talent and rewards it, but much of its first division is owned and controlled overseas. In that sense it is not in control of its destiny. It depends for its success on its critical mass, and if that ever started to unravel, nothing could save it.

Recovery and reinvention have done wonders for the City, but its greatest mistake would be to take its own success for granted. Its denizens should know by now that markets do not move in one direction for ever. Life is like that, and finance, after all, is human nature in action.

ACKNOWLEDGEMENTS

I am grateful to my colleagues, past and present, at *The Spectator* for their forbearance and, in particular, for enabling me to reprint excerpts from my City and Suburban column.

Martin Vander Weyer was confronted with a mountain of words and turned it into a book. Michael Alcock, as my agent, persuaded Nicholas Brealey to publish it, and Nicholas and his team allowed themselves to be persuaded. Mervyn King was kind enough to write a preface in terms more generous than I could deserve. My best thanks to them all.

Nigel Lawson first recruited me to write for *The Spectator* in the 1960s. Algy Cluff, chairman since 1980, suggested two decades ago that I should write a weekly column, and later invited me to join the board. Since then, as I have pointed out to him, the company's finances have changed for the better, though not necessarily as a matter of cause and effect. To him this book is dedicated.